COME AND SEE

COME AND SEE: THE JESUS APPROACH TO EQUIPPING BIBLICAL DISCIPLES

LISA SCHWARZ

Five Stones Press

COPYRIGHT

CONTENTS

Introduction   v

1. My Own Discipleship Experience   1
2. What is Discipleship?   16
3. Why is Discipleship important?   33
4. How Did Jesus Make Disciples?   48
5. The Discipleship Process in the Scriptures   66
6. Cultural Baptism   81
7. Being a Timothy First   87
8. What Does Being A Paul Require?   110
9. Generational Barriers   125
10. The Goal of Discipleship   136

Conclusion   153
Works Cited   155
About Crazy8 Ministries   157
About the Author   161
Also by Lisa Schwarz   163

INTRODUCTION

"Go therefore and make disciples of all the nations, baptizing them
in the name of the Father and of the Son and of the Holy Spirit,
teaching them to observe all things that I have commanded you;
and lo, I am with you always, even to the end of the age."
Matthew 28:19-20

God commissions us to "make disciples," and we know that
since He is the same yesterday, today and forever, His
commission has not changed...but our culture has! So, how
do we live out this commission in a way that can and will
be embraced in today's society?

   In today's Christian culture, I believe the concept of
discipleship has gotten lost. And, although most people
would agree with that statement, I feel that many do not
know why, nor do they know what to do about it.

   Many churches and ministries have strived to come up

with a "discipleship tool," but it is hard to stretch beyond the concept of Bible studies, small groups, life groups, Sunday School, etc. And, although these are all good things, most would agree that they are not accomplishing the task at hand. There was a time when we had many Bible studies offered through Crazy8 Ministries, but there was something missing. I have sat on many "discipleship committees" and have experienced much frustration as we pondered how to "chemically" create what SHOULD be happening organically in our Christian culture.

Once upon a time, older women lived with younger women, and they walked them through the daily living of motherhood, being a wife, walking with God, etc. And the same was true of the male populace, younger males sat under the teaching of older men to learn a trade...thus the concept of apprenticeship. We would all agree that it wasn't so much about learning the task at hand but rather the relationship.

It was through the relationship, the time that was spent together and the younger gleaning off the elder, that organic discipleship occurred, intimacy was developed, and lives were impacted and altered. If a grandmother spends time teaching her granddaughter how to make apple butter, that granddaughter is likely to continue making apple butter for years to come, not so much because they like the apple butter, but because it reminds them of their grandmother and what they learned from WHO grandma was. But with our many cultural changes, this has gotten lost.

We have become less and less relational and more and more technological resulting in a culture that is left to contend through life with much wandering and self-reliance. We have come to rely on learning information from books, manuals, messages, teachings, Google, education classes, etc., but the one-on-one "come along side you" concept has gotten lost. And unfortunately, with the business of our lives and the chaos in which we live, not only has it gotten lost, it seems no one has time for it.

So how do we take an age-old concept and flesh it out to fit today's society? It is this question along with my own discipleship experience that has compelled me to write this book.

I hope to put into these pages the discipleship concept that the Lord has taught me through my own discipleship experience, and through the years I have spent discipling others. I have been given the opportunity to teach and train on this concept, and it has proven to be a wonderful challenge to many to really look at their current attempts (or lack there of) at discipleship. I also plan to give practical "doing" examples to fill the gap from Biblical instruction to Biblical execution thus equipping and empowering us to fulfill the Great Commission to make disciples.

CHAPTER 1
MY OWN DISCIPLESHIP EXPERIENCE

I WAS SAVED at the age of 18 and by the time I was 21, I was 3 years married and had just had my first child. This was exactly what I always wanted but never realized how hard it would be. My first challenge was the postpartum depression from which I suffered. Adding to that challenge was that I did not have any idea what postpartum was and therefore I just thought I was losing my mind.

My second challenge was that Turner, our first child, was colicky and spent most of his days AND NIGHTS crying. That only compounded my feelings of inadequacy thus feeding the depression. I felt angry and deceived by the world. I had spent years watching sweet TV sitcoms and looking at pictures of mothers sitting in their rocking chairs holding their precious babies who quietly slept in their arms.

Realize that the settings of those pictures are typically in the middle of some kind of nursery that is clean and orderly …and so is mom! Her hair is perfect, her makeup is done, she appears peaceful and rested…and she is skinny!! Now, call me naive, but that was what I expected! I was sorely disappointed when that was not how it was for me. I fell apart emotionally, hormonally, and physically…but my fear of failure and feelings of inadequacy kept me from seeking help or crying out.

Although days would go by while I sat in my house with this newborn that I could not seem to satisfy, when I got in front of people, I found myself pretending to know what I was doing. I mean, let's face it, all the women around me had it all together. Women from all walks of life were having babies and handling life more gracefully than I was! This was the lie that I strived to perform under while secretly I was falling apart.

After struggling alone through my first round of postpartum, Brad and I had our second child, Maddison. Although she was completely different as a newborn, I still struggled with the depression. Only this time, my doctor picked up on the postpartum at her 2-week visit and prescribed anti-depressants. Although the meds helped me function, taking them somehow intensified only my feelings of failure.

My husband who was walking through a season of working full time, coaching to make "extra" money and also attending school was obviously unable to be at home a lot. In my eyes, and in my emotional instability, he "seemed" to be perfectly content to pursue life outside of our home. I found myself continuously feeling lonely and "unimportant." I now know that this was all my perception, but at the time it was very real.

I was unable to break free from my negative thinking and thoughts of worthlessness and lack of purpose, which caused me to live in a cycle of rejection...particularly self-rejection. In my continual "habit" of agreeing with these thoughts, it became my reality, which then became my identity. I developed standards that would help me succeed at the role of "Supermom" and "Superwife."

I mean, I graduated from high school early with a GPA of 4.3; surely I was smart enough to manage my home! But when I failed to meet these "self made" expectations, my self-abasement became more apparent. I responded to this rejection by settling into a pit, and I found myself not just struggling with postpartum, but with depression in general.

In the midst of all of this, I became a...well let's just say, "not so pleasant" wife to live with. I was unable to assess that my issues were my own issues and my husband was just an easy target, someone I could blame for my unhappiness and discontent. "If only he would let me catch a nap," or "If only he would help me around the house," or "If only he would take me on a date," then I would not feel the way I do and I would be able to accomplish more and be more "successful."

Neither Brad nor I had been raised in a Biblical environment, so we did not have any concept of what a Biblical marriage looked like. All we knew is that what was currently happening wasn't good. But, a lot of what I was struggling with was not just emotional issues; there was a lack of knowledge and training in so many areas of my life. While I was going to church on a regular basis, and was engaged in Bible studies, there seemed to be a "disconnect" on what all the information I was receiving looked like in action.

I had a lot of information, but there was no understanding of how to execute that information in my daily living. Little did I know that this lack of understanding was fueling my frustrations, feelings of inadequacy, and depression. All I knew was this "list of rules" that I had made for myself was now lengthened by the information I was learning from the church. Great, MORE standards that I was failing to live up to.

Once, I tried going to a Ladies' Bible study that met once per week. When I would FINALLY get my kids dressed, MYSELF dressed, the baby fed, the diaper bag packed, and everyone in the car, I was exhausted (mostly from yelling like a banshee to get that accomplished.) I would show up to the study with my "smile" only to feel like a failure, because I was unable to complete all of the daily assignments that the study required.

I remember one day I met with some church acquaintances at McDonald's with our kids for lunch. I cannot recall what exactly had happened that morning, but I know that I had come to a breaking point in my life. I felt like I was dying on the inside, and I was desperate for some genuine communion. I was realizing that I had spent the majority of my life faking it and pretending to be "ok" when I wasn't.

Pretending to have it all together when I didn't, pretending to be happy when I was deeply faint and weary. I did not realize it at the time, but, looking back now, I know it was the Holy Spirit that compelled me to drop the mask. Suddenly, I began to say out loud, "Do you guys ever feel lonely, or like nobody REALLY knows you? Do you ever wonder if you even know yourself? Or do you ever think about what you thought your life would look like and what it really looks like?

Do you ever feel so rejected by your husband that you think he wouldn't notice if you disappeared? Do you ever want to tell your mom to "shut up?" Do you ever feel like your mother in law will never find you worthy of being her son's wife? Do you ever feel like no matter how early you rise and how late you go to bed, your house will still be a mess? Do you ever cry the whole way to church, but then plant a big smile on your face when you get in the parking lot?"

I went on and on and on…and with each question I began to cry harder and harder. When I got finished spewing out these questions there was an awkward silence at the table. Although I felt emotionally like I had just undressed before these ladies, there was an incredible release. There was a freedom in being real, being honest, and just being me! Next thing I knew, these ladies all one by one began to cry as well. We spent the next 2 hours sharing how we all felt inadequate in so many ways and how we needed help!

It was at this lunch that these ladies and I collectively decided that we needed a "support group" at our church. A group that was helpful to us, yet practical. One that offered free babysitting, NO homework, and started AFTER 9:00am. And so the "Mom's Support Group" was birthed. It was in this group that I first experienced genuine sisterhood.

We came together every two weeks and we talked about real life stuff. We laughed, we cried, and sometimes we took naps!! I found company in these ladies as we connected in our season and the challenges it came with. We encouraged one another, we babysat for each other, we made meals for each other when our kids were sick, we shared discipline tips (and frustrations), and we fellowshipped.

We had great camaraderie within our support group, and I found it to be very fun and encouraging. But at some point, I became very aware that although we were all being encouraged, not many of us were actually learning or changing. The good thing was that we were all at the same place and could connect and relate in that place, but the problem was we could not help one another move from that place. It is kind of like the old adage of "the blind leading the blind."

Truth be told, looking back on it now, we often just "wallowed" with one another or connected in our complaints and frustrations. We would at times share tips of what worked and what didn't work, but for the most part it was just sharing information with one another.

Even when we would share encouraging, relevant Scriptures with one another, there was no concept of how to DO that Word. In other words, we were hearers of the Word, but not DOERS of the Word. (James 1:22) At some point, the Holy Spirit began to reveal to me the Biblical concept of the older teaching the younger.

"The older women likewise, that they be reverent in behavior, not slanderers, not given to much wine, teachers of good things – that they admonish the young women to love their husbands, to love their children, to be discreet, chaste, homemakers, good, obedient to their own husbands, that the word of God may not be blasphemed."
Titus 2:3-5

Ah yes! This was it, this was what I needed, and wanted...an older woman to invest into teaching me the Bible and what it says and what it means and how to live it daily. So I approached my "support group ladies" with this passage and suggested that we seek an older, "more seasoned" woman in the church to come in and start leading a Bible study for us. This was what I knew of discipleship, that you do Bible studies.

Don't get me wrong, I am NOT against Bible studies, but it cannot replace the concept of discipleship. And so we started our first study, and then the second, third, and so on. Now I do not intend to be negative, but I DO desire to be honest. What I found in starting these Bible studies was that they didn't do much more than teach me how to look up verses in the Bible and read the author's opinion and thoughts of that verse. I did, however, become more familiar with the locations of the books in the Bible and various key verses that I came to memorize, albeit out of context.

Starting the studies also trained me how to be somewhat disciplined in having a "quiet time" each day, albeit, only somewhat dutifully. But what the studies did NOT teach me was HOW to have fellowship with God, HOW to read the Bible or HOW to live it out. What I gained from those studies was a whole lot more information that I did not know what to do with…and remember my self imposed pressures? Well, learning all this information seemed to only highlight all the ways I was falling short and failing.

It was somewhere in the midst of the next 2 years that things would change for me profoundly in my relationship with God. The first thing was that I began singing in a group called The Kingdom Seekers, which started out with a group of 9 ladies who ministered through song. I spent the next 7 years of my life developing a sisterhood with these ladies, while at the same time memorizing Truths about God by singing them over and over.

I am not sure that even now I fathom the true depths of all the Lord did in me through that season and through those women. Singing the Word day after day as I practiced and practiced to learn what would end up to be some 40-50 songs in those years, thus imparting His Word into my heart and mind.

Little did I know that I was hiding His Word in my heart. We practiced every week for 2 hours, and we traveled to do "concerts" once a month. We shared so much together…struggles with our kids, with our husbands, with our finances…you name it, we shared it. But this group of ladies was different than I had previously experienced.

Although some were my same age, they had all been raised up in church and in the faith. And they were all not just church attendees, but they were engaged in the life of the church. They clearly lived differently than what I had known, and they challenged me in my walk. While some of them were older in the natural, all of them were older in the Spirit. I mention all of this to say, I was organically discipled by these ladies just by being around them. I have heard it called discipleship by immersion, but I like to think of it as a cultural baptism.

The second thing that happened around that time is that I got pregnant with our third child, Morgan. It was during my pregnancy that I began to have behavioral challenges with my 18 month old, Maddi. (You remember, that second child that was such an angel as a baby?!) I had no clue how to discipline her, and she was completely different than Turner. With the concern of knowing a newborn would soon be entering the scene, I sensed a desperation for help.

That is when I met Kate! I swear to this day that the Lord moved her and her family to Illinois just for me…

hehe. It is not that I am that selfish to think everything is about me, but I do know with confidence how much the Lord loves me and how even then He was working out His plan...and Kate was a huge part of that plan.

> *I remember Lisa calling and wanting to meet with the two of us and our husbands to talk about her unruly and strong-willed 18 month old. She had said she watched us in church and was quite fascinated with our family and she wanted to know what we knew about raising children. She was very nervous about how to cope with having the third child while her second child was so out of control. We talked for several hours about ways that they could begin to train their child to learn to obey and how to have a more cheerful household.*

I met Kate for the first time at the mom's group when she came to visit. She had just moved into town and started attending our church. Kate had 5 kids and was pregnant and there were several things that grabbed my attention about her (other than the amount of kids she had.) Kate was genuinely joyful, and I recall her children being obedient...and HAPPY. A pregnant mom of 5 kids who is at peace and her children were content.

Where did this family come from?!?! But here was the kicker...during the study, I remember the lesson being on intimacy with your husbands and the leader posed this question, "So ladies, what are your thoughts on sex?" WHAT?! We were in church for goodness sakes! There was a hush in the room and then suddenly Kate chimed in with a joyful, unashamed proclamation saying, "I really like it!" To this day, I tease her about that.

About a week later, we had a Mom's Group gathering and Kate was there. I could not take my eye off her. I am confident now that it was the Spirit of God that was drawing my eye to her and wooing my heart towards hers. Everything about her in the natural was completely the opposite of me, but everything about her intrigued me. I think I followed her around that night paying attention to every move she made and every word that came forth from her mouth. And the more I saw and heard, the more I was drawn in.

I don't think I have realized until possibly right now as I am typing exactly how powerfully the Spirit was moving to connect me to her. At some point that night, I started a conversation with her and it was in that conversation that I rubbed her arm...don't ask...but the point is I remember the softness of her skin. So I mentioned it, and her response was, "O, that's because I don't have any hair!" This woman just kept getting stranger and stranger, yet more intriguing.

The first time I ever saw Lisa was my first time visiting the church. She was part of a women's singing group that did special music that Sunday. She had a lovely voice and was very much a part of an 'in' group within the church.

I remember meeting Lisa at our church's Mom's Group about a month later. I was new to the church and pregnant with child #6. Most of the women in this group (except the leader) were in their early to mid-twenties and I was turning 40. They had babies and toddlers and I had been homeschooling for more than 6 years already. Most of them were young believers and I had been walking with the Lord for 20 years. While I was hoping to be ministered to in this group, God had plans of me ministering to others.

I remember the Christmas party where she touched my arm in conversation and noted how soft and smooth it was. I told her the reason was that I had no hair. It was quite humorous as she looked at my missing eyebrows and eyelashes, double checking I assume, and then took me around the room and had everyone stroke my arm while telling them I had no hair.

I remember her bringing me a meal when my baby was born and was shocked to find him lying on a blanket on the floor. "Aren't you afraid the other children will step on him?" I reassured her that it never happened as they were not allowed to step on the blanket at all. She was shocked that they actually obeyed.

When Morgan was born, Kate called me to set up a time to deliver a meal to our home. It was that phone call that opened the door to something that would last until today. I recall being tired and weary from birth and no sleep, being frustrated with the lack of "success" in my discipline tactics with my 2 year old, being filled with heaviness and despair because of postpartum, feeling angry because my husband got to sleep 8 hours straight, having nothing to wear, being overwhelmed with laundry and household duties, all while leaking out of every orifice in my body.

It was no doubt a Divine appointment when my phone

rang, and I heard a voice that I am now so familiar with that I can hear it in my head. She asked me when a good time would be to bring our meal, but then she pressed on and began to ask me other things…like, "How is the baby? Is she nursing well? How is she sleeping for you? How are your other children adjusting?" But she didn't stop there… she went on and began to ask about me, "Are you getting rest? How are your hormones? How is your appetite?" It was the first time that I had ever experienced someone inquiring about me after childbirth.

I guess you could say that she gave me permission to be real, and so I was. I began pouring out EVERYTHING, and by everything, I mean everything…no holding back…tears and all. Kate listened hard and then spoke back in a way that was new to me. She would not just address my challenge with a Scriptural Truth, but she would go on to connect to a real life example of what that Truth would look like executed in my home. For the first time, I was hearing a connection and seeing the relevance of the Word in my role as a mom and a wife. It was so refreshing…AND HELPFUL!! It is one thing to encourage someone; it is another to actually give them some practical tips.

I remember talking to Lisa on the phone a few months later, after her baby was born, and asking how she was. I heard all her fears and frustration, anxiety and anger pour out over the phone lines. My heart went out to this young mom struggling with all trials of being a new mom, dealing with post-partum depression and having several young children as well. I felt the Lord's

burden for her fill my soul. Thus began a relationship of almost
2 decades that went from child training and marital help to,
sometimes full-time, discipleship to mentoring and eventually
blossomed to a sweet friendship.

This was the beginning of what became a very intimate
relationship that I needed more than I knew at the time.
Kate helped me through so much over those years as I had
three more children, Carter, Moriah and Caden. The way
Kate spoke into me was exactly what I needed and it fit my
personality. There was always a little combination of
speaking in grace and truth…a Word of love and gentleness
with a "now get up and do this" twist thrown in. But our
relationship grew to be more than just a phone call where
she would instruct me.

It turned into her and I meeting once a week, sometimes
in her home and sometimes in mine. We would talk a lot,
but more than that, I observed and learned by watching her;
the way she spoke to her kids, the way she disciplined
them, the way she organized her meals, the way she
swaddled her newborns, etc. And she would watched me
as well, and then would instruct and correct and give
practical tips on ways to improve my walk in every aspect
of my life. To be honest, there was very little reading of the
Bible together and we have never done a Bible study…yet
our conversations were always saturated with Scripture.
She used stories, verses and characters from the Bible to
address almost every issue I was walking through. It was
organic and natural.

And these words which I command you today shall be in your heart. You shall teach them diligently to your children, and shall talk of them when you sit in your house, when you walk by the way, when you lie down, and when you rise up.
Deuteronomy 6:6 & 7.

I in no way have all the answers in regard to discipleship, nor do I claim to have it all figured out, but I do know what I was blessed to experience and how it worked for me. I also know that Kate's example compelled me to model the same concept in my own life for discipling others. I have been blessed to disciple a countless number of young ladies, moms, and women over the past 12 years; some to the extent of having them move into our home for a season.

This opened up the opportunity for a total baptism into the culture of our home. This requires MUCH transparency and vulnerability but has no doubt been the fastest and most effective form of discipleship that I have found.

I hope to share more about my relationship with Kate, as well as those I have discipled, throughout the pages of this book in order to capture what I think Biblical discipleship really looks like.

CHAPTER 2
WHAT IS DISCIPLESHIP?

OFTENTIMES WE ARE unable to receive new information, because we think we already know it. After all, this is what kept the Pharisees and Sadducees from receiving the "new wine" of which Jesus spoke. They thought they already had it figured out and there was an unwillingness to receive because there was an unwillingness to admit that they didn't already know it all. We see this concept explained by Jesus Himself in John 9 after the healing of the blind man.

And Jesus said, "For judgment I have come into this world, that those who do not see may see, and that those who see may be made blind." Then some of the Pharisees who were with Him heard these words, and said to Him, "Are we blind also?"

Jesus said to them, "If you were blind, you would have no sin; but now you say, "We see." Therefore your sin remains.
John 9:39-4

Jesus was, in a nutshell, saying, "Because you think you already know everything, you will not learn or receive anything new." Literally speaking, if my eyes are fixed on one spot, I cannot see anything else unless I first take my eyes off of that spot. This is the point Jesus is making. He is presenting them a new concept, but their unwillingness to consider something other than what they had always been taught was preventing them from receiving the Truth. In other words, they were not teachable, but rather, they were stuck in the rigidity of their old wine skin.

I am sharing all of this because one of the things that I think keeps us from walking in a Biblical picture of discipleship is that we think we already know what discipleship looks like. So before I go into what discipleship is…let me first tell you what it is not.

What Discipleship is Not

Here are some things that I think we define as discipleship: Sunday school classes, life classes, small groups, Bible studies (or book studies). Discipleship is not just about giving people information or feeding them answers and verses. Now, please do not think that I am saying that these are bad or purposeless, because that is certainly NOT what I am saying, nor do I feel that way. I am also not saying that some organic discipleship can't come forth from these things…in fact, if we are intentional, I think it can and often does. But what I am saying is this is not what I see when I look at the Biblical examples of discipleship.

Discipleship is also not just speaking Truths into people's lives, or instructing others. I will talk a lot more about this when I discuss relationships, but for now, know that it is much more than just telling people how to live their lives.

I challenge you as Jesus challenged His listeners when He would present them with some new information…to " Hearken and behold." Read with a desire to understand and receive, and look attentively with a desire to see and perceive.

Discipleship by Demonstration

So what is discipleship? Well let's break it down and first just intellectually look at some definitions. The word disciple in the Greek is the word, "mathetes, " which means, "learner" or "one who follows a teaching." It implies not just learning or following the teaching, but actually imitating the teacher. Here we see the concept of human-to-human interaction.

To be a disciple means that I don't just learn from a teaching, but rather I learn from THE teacher…a person. And I don't just learn from the information of the teacher but by imitation of the teacher. This is an important part of discipleship that I feel we often miss out on…imitation. It means there must be a person that lives a life that doesn't just speak, but also demonstrates and thus a disciple learns as they follow or imitate what the teacher is exemplifying.

But God demonstrates His own love toward us in that while we were still sinners, Christ died for us.
Romans 5:8

The very core of salvation was not simply spoken to us, it was DEMONSTRATED to us. It is so much easier for us to believe information when we see the heart of it through action. It is also easier for us to imitate when we see it played out through demonstration first. I often ask those around me after they speak a "concept" or a Truth from Scripture, "So what does that LOOK like?

And what would it look like for you to demonstrate that Truth in your life TODAY?" This is a question that is intended to move us from a place of knowledge to a place of wisdom, where we know how to take knowledge and apply it to our lives. This is further presented throughout the Proverbs when Solomon talks about not just "getting understanding," but also "getting wisdom." He talks about both because understanding is simply the knowledge and perception of an idea or concept, while wisdom is the application of it.

It is noteworthy to mention that the word demonstrate in Romans 5:8 is interpreted in the KJV as "commendeth" in the English. In the Greek it means, "To place together, to set in the same place, to bring or band together." In other words, God's love lined up with His action. There was no "disconnect," because His love and His action were brought together through the death of His son.

I mentioned that I struggled for years in having head knowledge and a knowing of the Scriptures, but having no clue how that knowledge was either relevant or applicable to my daily living. Even when I did see the relevance, I did not know how to "play it out" and actually connect knowledge to action. Though I had knowledge, I was unable to move into a life of wisdom.

Moving From Knowledge to Wisdom

What do we learn about the heart of God from Romans 5:8? We learn that God loves by demonstrating sacrificially even to those who are unworthy. So what is God saying to mankind? He is saying that we, being created in HIS image, also should demonstrate love by sacrificing...even to those who don't deserve it. Most of us would stop examining this Truth at this point and would move on, but let's dig deeper and really allow this verse to probe us and challenge us.

I want to move beyond knowledge and into wisdom. So let's go further and ask these next questions. "What does demonstrating a sacrificial love LOOK like practically? What does it LOOK like for a mom who is at home everyday raising kids? Or for one who is in the workplace? Or for the student who is in school? Let's bunker down here and hash this out…I want to know how God's demonstration connects to us everyday and what it LOOKS like played out.

It is hard to know what that looks like if I have never seen it through another person's life. I need to have this demonstrated for me through a real live human! This is why having more than information is so important, we MUST get back to relationships that allow others to see and watch and learn. This is what shifts us from having understanding to walking in that understanding, which is wisdom.

From Information to Execution

There is more than just information in discipleship. More than just a spoken word, information or sitting through a teaching is necessary. True discipleship involves recognizing that information is not enough, but performance is essential. It is moving someone from a place of knowledge to a place of execution. Discipleship is not simply a matter of how much you know. It is vitally concerned with how much you can do.

But be doers of the word and not hearers only, deceiving yourselves. For if anyone is a hearer of the word and not a doer, he is like a man observing his natural face in a mirror; for he observes himself, goes away and immediately forgets what kind of man he was. But he who looks into the perfect law of liberty and

continues in it, and is not a forgetful hearer but a doer of the
work, this one will be blessed in what he does."
James 1:22-25

When we choose to simply hear the word but not DO the word, we are deceiving ourselves. It is in DOING the word that we demonstrate the truth of who we really are. Interestingly enough, this is also God's way of sanctifying us so that we can live out the fullness of His identity in us. In other words, what we say we know and believe needs to be seen in the way we live our life. This is where we have to have integrity.

If we say we believe something, but there is no proof through our actions, then our knowledge is useless. We would all agree that actions speak louder than words, and now we know it is actually a Biblical Truth. One of the reasons why Christians are often characterized as being hypocrites is because we don't demonstrate a life in Christ. We know it, we talk about it, and we certainly preach it, but are we living it?!

We use a mirror to "get ready," or prepare for the day. We need a mirror to make sure we look appropriate...that our hair is in place, that our face is clean, to apply our make-up, shave our face...we are using the mirror to better our appearance. It reveals everything about our appearance, every spot and every wrinkle, and without a mirror we would never know what we look like.

That is the purpose of a mirror...to see ourselves and know what we look like and to examine ourselves so that we can be sure that we are presentable. So it is with the Word of God! It is through the Word that we learn what we look like. However, it is not to just have knowledge of what we look like but also to be used to refine us and adjust us, remold us and remake us. It is through the Word that God desires to reveal the Truth of who we really are and to sanctify us into that Truth.

No doubt when we stand in front of a mirror, it typically prompts an action with the motive of becoming more presentable. This is what this passage is saying metaphorically. The Word should prompt action in our lives that makes us more presentable thus representing Christ more effectively to the world. AND, if we continue to walk in the Word even after we close the book, this passage promises that we will be blessed. Look closely at verse 25; it says we will be blessed by what we do, not what we know.

James expounds on this in chapter 2.

What does it profit, my brethren, if someone says he has faith but does not have works? Can faith save him? If a brother or sister is naked and destitute of daily food, and one of you says to them, "Depart in peace, be warmed and filled," but you do not give them the things which are needed for the body, what does it profit? Thus also faith by itself, if it does not have works, is dead.

But someone will say, "You have faith, and I have works." Show me your faith without your works, and I will show you my faith by my works. You believe that there is one God. You do well. Even the demons believe—and tremble! But do you want to know, O foolish man, that faith without works is dead? Was not Abraham our father justified by works when he offered Isaac his son on the altar? Do you see that faith was working together with his works, and by works faith was made perfect?

Again, we see that there is a call to connect our knowledge to our action; to move from information to execution. "Faith working together with his works;" there should be no disconnect but rather a coming together or lining up of word and deed. We can have all the faith in the world, but if we don't demonstrate it through action, what is the point of it? Our personal faith is purposeless and frankly ineffective if it is not seen in the way we live our lives.

I know your works, that you are neither cold not hot. I would wish you were cold or hot. So then, because you are lukewarm, and neither cold not hot, I will vomit you out of My mouth."
Revelation 3:15-16

This passage is not referring to your faith, but rather your "works," or your actions and the effectiveness of them. I want to be careful because God desires works compelled by the Holy Spirit and not by the flesh. But the point is in Bible times, hot springs were used for medicinal purposes and cold springs were used for refreshment. There was a purpose to hot and cold water, but lukewarm water was yucky and stagnant. There was no medicinal value, and if you were to drink it you would probably spit it out.

I fear that we have become selfish Christians, and we

have made our faith about us instead of about the Kingdom. We have our faith, but we struggle to do anything with it, in other words, we have not works. We run the risk of becoming what may be called fat and selfish faith hoarders who are ineffective and unproductive. This is why much of the world has deemed us (the church) as irrelevant and useless to them. So knowledge of who God is (faith) without action (works) will amount to nothing and will bear no fruit for the Kingdom.

So let's connect this to life…

I can have all the information in the world, but if I do not know how to execute that information into action, what good is it? I may know the greatest recipe for the best cake, but if I don't know how to execute the recipe into action and actually bake the cake, I will never reap the reward of tasting it. Furthermore, if I have never been in a kitchen before, I need someone to come along side me to demonstrate HOW to measure things, HOW to combine my ingredients, and HOW to tell if the cake is actually done.

Think about it, if you are going in for heart surgery, do you want a surgeon who has just read up on heart surgery? Maybe he knows the names of the parts of your heart, and all the surgical tools…or maybe has even watched the surgery on YouTube or during a class that he has taken. Is that information of heart surgery enough for you? Not for me! I want a surgeon who has more than information. I want a surgeon who has not just SEEN it done, but was also trained in the surgical room by another heart surgeon. This is a no brainer.

Let's consider the concept of "See one, do one, teach one." This is what the medical field has adopted in teaching their nurses. Before they get their license, they have seen, done and taught medical procedures. I think it is understood that before they see it, do it and teach it, they have read up on it in a textbook and have no doubt learned general information in some kind of classroom setting.

Think about getting an IV. Before a nurse can do an IV on you or me, they have read up on it in a textbook, they have been given instructions by an instructor, they have seen it demonstrated for them, they have done it themselves, and then they have turned around and taught another how to do it. I don't know about you, but I am glad for that picture of discipleship when I am on the receiving end of that IV!

Many occupations use this same concept: lawyers, teachers, CPAs, mechanics, etc. But I do not often see this concept in the Kingdom. We will discuss some of the reasons why we don't see it in the chapters to come, but for now we just need to expose the problem and agree that we aren't doing it. Remember, we can't embrace something new if we are not willing to accept that we don't have it figured out. All of this is to say I have learned that if the mechanism of discipleship does not move us from a place of information to execution, the process is failing.

Discipleship Requires Activity

A quote I once read said this, "Discipleship is the

intensely personal activity of two or more persons helping each other experience a growing relationship with God." There are some key words I would like to point out in this quote: let's look at the word activity. Webster defines the word activity as, "The state of being active, energetic action or movement; liveliness." Ok, so I am already seeing a distinct difference between this and what we would typically consider discipleship, yes? So let's add the words "intensely personal" to activity.

This implies doing more than just talking or chatting with one another, but rather there is some activity happening between them; there is movement, energetic action, and liveliness in this relationship! Here is one thing that I have learned…discipleship is a verb! It is an action word and requires activity and DOING things. This goes back to what we discussed on demonstration. There is activity and movement involved in demonstration. In general, because of the convenience of modern technology, we have become an inactive culture. We don't even need to get up to answer the phone anymore.

The ingenuity of man has spoiled us and it has bred into us a real lack of movement. Once upon a time, we didn't need fitness centers because people moved their body in their work. I often say that people have good intentions, but they aren't intentional, and there is a difference between having intention and being intentional. Being intentional means I am going to demonstrate my intentions through action. I am not just going to talk about it, but I am going to DO it.

*For a dream comes through much **activity**, And a fool's voice is known by his many words.*
Ecclesiastes 5:3

The Bible uses the word activity in this verse to differentiate between those who achieve their dreams and those who do not. It says that a fool is one who simply talks a lot. Are you seeing a theme here? I sure am! Let's press into the word "activity" in this verse. The KJV says, "A multitude of business" instead of activity, which frankly sounds a little less "fun" if you will. It comes from the Hebrew word, "inyan" which means occupation, task, or job.

The word is found eight times in the old testament and is actually interpreted into the English word "travail" six of those eight times. So...what does this mean and how does it connect to discipleship? It means discipleship requires an active work. It means I am going to often wear myself out for the sake of pouring into another person. It means I am going to love them "In deed and in truth."

My little children, let us not love in word or in tongue, but in deed and in truth.
1 John 3:18

Hear me when I say this, salvation takes but a moment, but discipleship takes a lifetime...and it requires dedication and work. I can go around all day long poking holes in

hearts and planting seeds, but it is the harvesting of the
field that requires sweat equity.

More Than Verbal Ministry

When Crazy8 Ministries first started, I traveled and
ministered the gospel by preaching and teaching in all
kinds of arenas…churches, prisons, youth camps, business
workshops, etc. And though I still do, there came a time in
my life when the Lord asked me what I was really doing to
love His people. He wasn't saying that I didn't love people,
but rather He was asking me how I was the demonstrating
love for others on a daily basis?

Now, I am not knocking people who travel and simply
speak, that may indeed be the course the Lord has set for
them. But, the Lord had another course for me, and He
brought me to a place personally where I was no longer
satisfied with just ministering the gospel verbally. He
allowed a discontent to rise up in me because He was
calling me to do more. There were many things that He
began to develop in Crazy8 as an extension to the
conference ministry that required more than just weekend
travels or fun filled retreats. He started by birthing the
Counseling Ministry and then the Discipleship Ministry,
which organically came forth from the conferences.

They were a natural extension of how we could continue
ministering to those I had encountered at these conferences
who needed more help. But when I sensed that He wanted
me to open a home for women and their children to come

for a season of restoration and discipleship, I was like…"
Uhhhhh, no thank you." I am just being honest with you! I
was already starting to get bogged down with the "burden"
of ministering daily as well as the burden of the logistical
side of developing a non-profit ministry. Remember, I had
been a stay at home mom, who homeschooled, so I was
used to being able to sit in my PJs all day if I wanted. I
remember fussing at God when I realized the amount of
work and dedication it was going to require to restore
women (and their children) who were broken in every
aspect of their lives and had been for most of their lives.

Finally, one morning I broke down and threw myself a
bit of a temper tantrum. I shook my fists and begged Him
to pick someone else, pleading my case and saying that I
just wanted to travel and speak…that having all these other
aspects to the ministry would just "weigh me down." I will
never forget His response to me as He lovingly reminded
me of how He too loved those times when He got to stand
in front of the multitudes and preach. That He could relate
to connecting with a crowd of people and ministering the
Word. But then He reminded me that He also carried a
cross for those people and that without the weight of that
cross upon His back and the work that it accomplished, the
gospel would not have been complete.

Those are the moments when you move very quickly
from a state of shaking your fists at God to throwing
yourself on the floor, face down and repenting. I realized
that the Lord was trying to complete Crazy8's gospel
ministry by extending ourselves to the homeless. Until

then, we had ministered to many who were sick in their soul, but not to those who were in a sick circumstance. I quickly loosed my fists and surrendered everything. It was after that, that I began to feel so burdened by the need for a shelter in our area that I would stop at nothing until it was built.

So He (Jesus) answered and said, "You shall love the lord your God with all your heart, with all you soul, with all your strength, and with all your mind," and your neighbor as yourself.
Luke 10:27

Loving With Your Strength

I often think we skim right over the part of this verse about loving the Lord with all your strength. Am I just going to love in word, or will I engage actively and invest energy and sweat equity into the Kingdom; God's people? Loving with your strength means I am going to work in the field (the lives of people) on the hot days and on the cold days…in the sun and in the rain. This is what it means to disciple others. Look, let's be honest, people can be very difficult to deal with…especially those who have settled into a state of brokenness.

Some of the manifestations of those who are broken are rebellion, self-pity, disrespect, an unwillingness to be loved or helped combined with a lack of social skills, life skills, hygiene skills, etc. I am not just talking about the ladies in our home; I am talking about you and me. We all have places in our lives where we struggle with brokenness or what we call "sickness" that results in a very unattractive behavior. I cannot tell you how many times I was ugly to Kate because of hurt I was dealing with, or sin I was hiding. I knew that she could see it and so I would put up a defense that often appeared like a cobra ready to strike.

It would have been so easy for her to throw her hands up and say, "I am done with you Lisa!" But thank goodness the love of God in her poured out in the form of longsuffering. It was her demonstration of God's relentless love to me that now compels me to do the same for others. I learned by hearing more than just words and gaining information but by seeing information executed in the form of actions.

CHAPTER 3
WHY IS DISCIPLESHIP IMPORTANT?

I AM one who loves to ask questions. I think that we can often learn more through questions than we can through answers. The problem is that we are often afraid to ask questions...I know that my soul does not care for when someone asks me questions. I have some people on my staff that are very detailed in everything, and as a visionary, I am not into the details, I am into the big picture.

The details just bog me down and tend to discourage me because they can be overwhelming. I tend to feel like when someone is asking questions they are "poking holes" in the vision and squelching my dream, or that they are questioning me personally. But as I have grown with Crazy8, I have learned that the Lord has used these people to challenge me to really work out the visions He gives.

I have come to appreciate that sometimes they ask questions that NEED to be asked and they see things that

NEED to be considered. Now, let me remind you that these people are in a position in my life where they have "the right" to ask me questions...like board members or ministry council members.

As a counselor, that is what I do...I ask questions. I often tell people that being an effective counselor is not about having great answers but rather asking great questions. When a client tells me something, I ask a question for the purpose of challenging them to think through what they just said, why they said it, what they are going to do with it, etc. I ask and ask for the purpose of stretching that person out of their typical "thinking cycle" and getting them to think in a new direction.

I think we would do well to welcome questions and challenge ourselves in the Kingdom to think outside of our typical "thinking cycle." So, before we go on in looking at the Biblical concept of discipleship, let's ask, "Why?" "Why is discipleship so important?"

The Great Commission

Well, the obvious first response to that is because God commands it.

Go therefore and make disciples of all nations, baptizing them in the name of the Father and of the Son and of the Holy Spirit. Teaching them to observe all things that I have commanded you...
Matt. 28:19-20

We call this the "Great Commission"…the final exhortation or instruction that Jesus gives to His own disciples; that they are to go and do likewise, which is to make disciples. But that is not all; He says to teach them to observe all things that I have commanded you. This requires more than just conversions. Remember, salvation takes only a moment, but discipleship takes a lifetime. It is easy to get caught up in the ministry to the masses where many come forward, but God began to show me that you really reach the masses by touching one person at a time.

One of the reasons why I started our Biblical Counseling/Discipleship Ministry was because I was tired of leading people to Christ but not empowering individuals to walk with Christ. The Bible says we are to "Work out our salvation" (Phil. 3:12), and that requires discipleship.

In John 11, we read about the death and resurrection of Lazarus. I love this passage because it further demonstrates the command to disciple others.

Now when He (Jesus) had said these things, He cried with a loud voice, "Lazarus, come forth!" And he who had died came out **bound hand and foot with graveclothes, and his face was wrapped with a cloth. Jesus said to them, (the disciples) "Loose him, and let him go."**

What a beautiful picture of how it is with our God. In a moment, He supernaturally resurrects people simply by calling their name and brings them forth to life through salvation. But just like Lazarus, even after that new life, there are things that still keep us bound; "graveclothes" that still bind us up. We are bound by anger, or depression, or addiction, or fear, or pride and so on and so on.

Lazarus' graveclothes posed to keep him stumbling and fumbling in the dark EVEN AFTER SALVATION and threatened to steal the fullness of life that Jesus intended for him in his resurrection. I need you to get this! This is a picture of those who have simply received salvation but have no discipleship. They are too often still bound by their past, and by their sick thinking and sick emotions…which leads them into sick choices and lands them in sick circumstances. The point is this, Jesus Himself could have walked over and removed those burial cloths, but He didn't. Instead He looked at His disciples and said, "Loose him, and let him go."

The call is the same to us today. All over our culture, we see evidence of what we call "sick Christians" who are indeed saved but are bound by all kinds of stuff. We must hear the voice of Jesus saying, "Hey, someone set these people free! For whom the Son has set free is free indeed!" (John 8:36) We should be so lined up with the Father's heart that we are vexed by seeing our brothers and sisters who have been set free yet are still bound up by burial cloths. This vexing should compel us to step in and come alongside them on behalf of their freedom. We need to understand that this is a stewardship that God has entrusted to us; a stewardship of discipleship.

If anyone comes to Me and does not hate his father and mother,
wife and children, brothers and sisters, yes and his own life also,
he cannot be My disciple. And whoever does not bear his cross
and come after Me cannot be My disciple. For which of you,
intending to build a tower, does not sit down first and count the
*cost, **whether he has enough to finish it – lest after he has***
laid the foundation, and is not able to finish, all who see it
begin to mock him.
Luke 14:26-29 (Emphasis mine)

I have put this verse in context so you can hear that part of
the call of being a disciple is more than just laying the
foundation of salvation in lives, but rather building up lives
after salvation is established. This is discipleship. Consider
the grave consequences that are spoken of in this passage
when we don't complete what we start...mockery. If we
were honest, we would all agree that Christians are very
much mocked for the same reasons.

We lead people to Christ and people hear that, but when
they see no changes in that person's life, they mock us.
"And he calls himself a Christian!" We, as believers, even
sometime fall into that same mentality in the form of
judgment or criticism of that person, yet we are the ones
who are failing to build into their lives.

Ok, going back to the concept of learning through
questions, we want to teach ourselves to allow the
Scriptures to challenge us and so I often will take passages
like these and ask myself some questions. In regard to the
great commission, what does it look like to "go"? Am I

making disciples or am I making converts…or am I doing either? Am I investing in people after I lead them to Christ? OK, how about asking these same questions of the body of Christ and of churches?

I am probably about to step on some toes here, but again, I am not afraid to ask some good questions…so let's "go there" and pose some questions specifically to today's church institution. Are we as a body more interested in making churches or making disciples? Are we more interested in developing programs than we are people? Are we building walls or are we building bridges? Is our goal to get people into our church or to get them into the Kingdom? Is our goal to touch people or transform them?

Are our "really cool" programs working? And by working I mean are they making disciples NOT just getting attenders. I am NOT bashing the church, but I am asking questions. I do not desire to dishonor the church, but I do desire to challenge the church. Why do we do what we do? Have you ever taken the time to ask yourself every year BEFORE you spend your time, money and energy on an annual "tradition" to consider the fruit of the years before? Or to ask God if that tradition is still relevant to this year and today's culture?

I am not saying that I am against traditions or that we should stop doing them, but I AM saying that we should be willing to. If I had a quarter for every time I have heard someone say, "Because this is the way we have always done it," I would be a rich woman. Funny thing is, often these people don't even know why or what started it.

In the business world, there is a lot of talk about return on investment, or ROI for short. I have learned as the Founder of Crazy8 to consider financially what kind of return I will get on every marketing investment. I have the responsibility of stewardship over every penny that comes in, and I take that very seriously. So, I will research things out and ask myself, or others, questions before I invest. And then when I do, I carefully and prayerfully consider the return.

If I do not see that the money was wisely spent, then I stop investing in that. Sounds simple right? Well, let's apply that spiritually to our lives and to the kingdom. Every minute, every ounce of energy, every penny, and every gift that I have has been first given to me. These are talents and seeds that the Lord has entrusted to me. They are not mine to spend, but rather they are His given for me to invest into His people and His Kingdom. Let's not put the words "talents" or "seeds" in a box but rather consider the fullness of what they include and how they apply to us in our daily lives. In other words, the reference to seeds or talents can be our time, our energy, our money, our resources, our wisdom, our gifts, etc.

In the parable of the sower (Mark 4), we often look at that passage and make it all about the soil that is being sown into. But recently I heard the Lord challenging me to consider the responsibility of the sower, and I sensed Him telling me to consider the seed as anything that He has given me to sow. If I continue to sow my seed of time, money, energy, gifts, and just resources in general into places where I see no fruit, at what point do that become my fault as the sower?

I need to back up and prayerfully consider where I am sowing my seed and whether or not I am just continuing to throw it along the wayside, which for a farmer would be considered a waste. I need to take some ownership of that and ask myself why I continue to pour into a place where I see no fruit even after seasons of sowing. Now hear me when I say this, we always reap in a different season in which we sow, and therefore we do indeed need to be willing to sow for a season even though we may not see any fruit.

Galatians 6:9 says, "And let us not grow weary while doing good, for in due season we shall reap if we so not lose heart." The point is, there is a great deal of discernment that needs to be practiced in knowing where to sow and how much to sow, and how long to sow in that place. But as a steward, we need to constantly consider the ROI for the Kingdom, and this means I need to ask myself questions and not just keep doing what I have been doing without prayerful consideration.

I recently found myself very stretched in all of the opportunities that are out there for Crazy8 as well as the things that I have gotten involved with to build for our community. Being three years into the ministry, it was time for me to step back and re-evaluate before the Lord. There were many things that were pulling me into places that I found draining, and I was feeling trapped by my schedule. I have to take responsibility for that myself. Kate has always said, "Lisa, there is always time to do the will of God." And she is right.

If I know what God has told me to do, then the resources to accomplish that will not be a problem. So I had to go back to the Lord and consider the things and places He wanted me to sow into versus the places that others (or I myself) wanted me to sow into. This book is an example. I know that God had told me in January that He wanted me to focus on writing this book and so I put a weekly timeframe to repeat in my calendar for the entire year.

The problem is that as of March 15 I had not even started, because every week something had "come up" that urged my time. This is just one example of how I was allowing myself to be thrown off course and get distracted by urgencies and "have to's." I was stretched thin and finding myself being tossed back and forth by people, meetings, events, "opportunities," etc. Now, many of these things God once had told me I was to be involved in, but, now 3 years later, He was calling me to consider the "ROI" for the Kingdom. It was in that moment that He took me to the parable of the sower and then said, "It is time to pick up your seed bag and move to the richest soils."

Our God is intentional and strategic. He doesn't just thoughtlessly scatter His seed all over the place, and He desires us to be the same. We should be very intentional and strategic in where we sow our seed, how we sow it, how much we sow it and how long we sow it. So I say all this to ask these questions, "Are we being intentional about the great commission?" "Are we being strategic in making disciples?" "What kind of ROI are we getting…NOT in our churches, but in the Kingdom?"

I can't help but wonder how the body of Christ would change if we were as intentional about sowing into people as we are about sowing into our buildings and our programs and our media productions. What if we launched more people instead of launching more programs, what if we promoted Jesus instead of promoting our churches or our ministries…just some questions, that's all! I am not saying that we cannot use these things for the purpose of making disciples, but it is always good to ask and re-evaluate and consider whether or not it is working.

If we were honest, often our motives get skewed and our resources get wasted. Times are changing and so are people…what always worked may not work today and what we think might work might not work at all. I am all about trying new ideas, but where are the checks and balances? It is in the question…are we making disciples? Are we fulfilling the great commission?

Surviving vs. Thriving

Discipleship is important because it is what teaches us to thrive and not just survive. It is easy to feed a man a fish, but teaching them to fish is a whole other ballgame. In other words, giving people advice and telling them what the Word says is different from teaching them how to hear from the Lord for themselves. Discipleship is moving someone into the "victorious tomorrow" phase of life…

where you teach someone HOW to seek his or her own intimacy with God and therefore gain wisdom for victorious daily living. This is different than just holding their hand through a current need or crisis.

One of the things that I loved about homeschooling my kids was that I did not have time (or frankly the knowledge) to teach them all they needed to know. So instead, I simply taught them how to seek and find information. I remember the first day Turner went to school. His teacher, who was originally skeptical on his ability to survive her class since he was homeschooled, shared this story with me. Seventh grade, and they were instructed to name the five parts of speech. She said they could work together or do whatever they needed to do to come up with the answer.

Turner did not know the answer nor did any of the other kids in the class. As they all worked together trying to think of the 5 parts, Turner got up and asked the teacher if he was allowed to use the dictionary. Guess what?! He found the answer! This is a great picture of what discipleship is about…it is teaching people how to seek and find God for themselves and engage in their own relationship with Him.

God created us to thrive, not to survive. We see words in the Bible like flourish, blessings, prosper, success, favor, increase, abundance, life, overflow, more than enough, double portion, more the conquerors, etc. These are words that indicate thriving. We would do well to understand the fullness of what is due to us so that we would not stop short of the promise land and settle for the wilderness.

Listen, there is a difference between being free and being free indeed. One is a release from Egypt while the other is being ushered into the land flowing with milk and honey! For us to feed people answers and not teach them how to find answers is not empowering them to step into their own relationship with the Lord and lean on the Holy Spirit for themselves. Doing that will, at best, keep them circling in the wilderness managing from crisis to crisis. I often tell people that there is a big difference between surviving our season and mastering our season.

Discipleship is when we teach others how to master their season...how to sing praise in the midst of captivity like Paul and Silas did and completely rely upon God to show up for them. Trust me, you can survive your seasons all you want, but until you learn to master your seasons, God will keep them coming back around...been there!

Honestly, often our own pride will keep people reliant upon us because often we like being needed, and we don't want people to become self-sufficient. We may not recognize this overtly, but it is true. I see it in parents with their children, among friends, and in counselors with their clients. It's a bit of the martyr syndrome where we want to fix everything for others and be their martyr. This will not help others move into a place of thriving but rather relying on us to feed them. Remember we talked earlier about how discipleship is not just giving people answers or feeding them information...and this is why, because it does not help people move into their tomorrow but rather only helps them survive their today.

The ladies in our Welcome Home Ministry come to us in survival mode. And if you knew some of their stories and the circumstances that they are trapped in, you would applaud their survival. However, I am not satisfied with survival...because God is not satisfied with survival.

I want to see these ladies thrive and come into the fullness that God intends for them. I want to see them live up to all they have attained in Christ. (Phil. 3:16) This requires us to teach them how to think and make intentional decisions. They tend to make choices that will get them through the moment, and our job is to ask them questions that will challenge their thinking cycle. I want them to stop thinking about the here and now and start thinking further ahead...into their tomorrow. We call it "thinking long."

This is a new thinking cycle for them because they have never been in a position practically where they could afford to think about tomorrow because they needed food or shelter for today. Part of my heart behind the Welcome Home Ministry is to offer a season of rest from life's circumstances so that they can make wise and intentional decisions instead of urgent and desperate decisions. You have no idea how hard it is to shake them out of that thinking cycle, and feeding them answers doesn't do it. It is done through asking them questions and challenging them to think and be intentional.

Jesus Made Disciples

So, why else is discipleship so important? Simply said, because Jesus did it! If Jesus did it, so should we. Consider what Jesus spoke in the book of John.

I have glorified You on the earth. I have finished the work which You have given Me to do…I have manifested Your name to the men whom You have given Me out of the world…
John 17:4&6

Notice that Jesus stated here that He had finished the work the God had given Him to do BEFORE He climbed the hill to Calvary, before the crucifixion, and before the resurrection. So what "work" was He referring to? The work of making disciples! I think we downplay or rather completely dismiss this, yet making disciples was a huge part of Jesus' purpose here on earth. He was to make manifest the name of God to the men God chose for Him. He was to make disciples…how? By demonstrating and manifesting the Word of God.

And the Word became flesh and dwelt among us, and we beheld His glory, the glory as of the only begotten of the Father, full of grace and truth."
John 1:14

The point is that we don't realize or emphasize that in everything Jesus was doing, He was intentionally doing it with His disciples in mind. Read the gospels and look specifically for the interaction between Jesus and the disciples. Take note not just of the miracles, but also of the disciples during the miracles.

Notice their proximity to Jesus, their involvement in His work, the interactions between them and Jesus. Think about how many times the Bible says something about the disciples "who were with Him." They were always with Him, and Jesus was always aware that they were watching and learning. Consider where they were standing, what they were thinking, and how they were learning by observing His every move.

The way they were transformed was not just by what He did but also by who He was. Jesus was not ignorant to their childlike eyes watching His every move, nor was He ignorant to their questions, fears, and doubts. He was intentional and strategic in all that He did, much for the purpose of developing His disciples.

God's commandment of the Great Commission, His heart for us to come into a life of fullness, combined with the emphasis that Jesus placed on His work of making disciples, should compel us to do the same. We must grasp the importance of discipleship and be willing to make changes to accomplish this. It is at the very core of the Father's heart for us to pour into people and be willing to build more than just foundations. So let's start hashing out what this looks like practically.

CHAPTER 4
HOW DID JESUS MAKE DISCIPLES?

SO LET'S focus on the Scriptures and take a look at the way Jesus raised up His disciples.

And Jesus, walking by the Sea of Galilee, saw two brothers, Simon called Peter, and Andrew his brother, casting a net into the sea; for they were fisherman. Then He said to them, "Follow Me, and I will make you fishers of men."
Matthew 4:18&19

There are many things that we can learn just from these two verses, but let me home in on two points. First, we see here that Jesus states the purpose of discipleship. He is not just picking men to follow Him, but He is letting them know what His intentions are with their lives. He wants to make them "fishers of men." In other words, He doesn't just want them to come to Him, but He wants to turn them into men who go get others and reproduce for the Kingdom. The word, "make" here in the Greek means, "to produce, to make ready, to prepare, to bear, to shoot forth… to lead him out, to put one forth…" these are just some of what this word encompasses.

But, the point is Jesus' full intention in reaching out to the disciples was to make them ready, to shoot them forth, to make them productive, and they knew this at the call. What if we had that same intention every time we reached out to someone? This encompasses more than just salvation, but a pouring into their lives through discipleship so that they can reproduce effectively for the Kingdom.

Now, I am not saying that we are called to disciple everyone; even Jesus didn't disciple every person with whom He came in contact. However, we ARE called to disciple. But let's be honest, we are lucky if we see believers actively discipling even one person.

Follow Me

The second thing I want to home in on is Jesus' call to His disciples seen in His words "Follow Me" throughout the Scriptures. The phrase "Follow me" in the Greek is "akoloutheo," meaning to accompany, assist, or be in the same way. This is where the term "acolyte" comes from, which is an alter server in the Catholic Church. An acolyte is called to accompany, assist, and be in the same way with the priest at all times for the purpose of helping the priest. But in this process, the acolyte is organically taught and trained how to be a priest himself. He is discipled by the priest organically through his position and service.

Let's break this concept down even more.

To Accompany

And HE went up on the mountain and called to Him those He Himself wanted And they came to Him.
Mark 3:13

———

And it happened, as He was alone praying, that His disciples joined Him...
Luke 9:18

———

Then He went out from there and came to His own country, and His disciples followed Him.
Luke 6:1

———

Now Jesus and his Disciples went out to the towns of Caesarea Philippi...
Mark 8:27

There are so many verses that could be listed here, but read the gospels for yourself, and take note of how many times the Scripture clearly states that the disciples were WITH Jesus. Everywhere He went, they went.

When people ask me what one of the major components to discipleship is, I say, "Take them with you." This is a very simple and easy way to disciple, and it doesn't take any time because you are still going about your business, doing what you need to do, and your disciples are just with you.

People in our community are used to seeing me with our interns, but what I am doing is discipling. I will home in on the one or two that the Lord has assigned to me for that season, and I will take them to all my meetings, luncheons, errands, etc. They typically spend a lot of time in my home, accompanying me in all that I am doing. This throws in the element of being baptized by a culture. Anytime we spend a lot of time around a particular culture, we automatically pick up on their language, their attitudes, their belief system, etc. and so it can be with discipleship.

When your disciple is just accompanying you in your everyday life, they will organically pick up on your attitude, your language, the way you discipline your kids, or talk about your spouse, the way you respond to offense, how you address a conflict and so on and so on. This is my favorite form of discipleship, because it is easy. It takes no time or energy away from what I need to do, in fact when you learn to let them assist you, it can be a great help!

To Be In the Same Way With

This leads us nicely right up to the part of "follow me" that encompasses "being in the same way with." You and I both know that it is possible to follow someone, but not be in the same way with them. It is important to note that Jesus not only was calling the disciples to follow Him, but to be one with Him, body, soul and spirit. He wanted them to think like He thought, desire what He desired, love what He loved, hate what He hated, and to have an overall understanding of the heart of God and be in line with it. We see an example of this in the garden of Gethsemane.

*Coming out, He went to the Mount of Olives, as He was accustomed, **and His disciples followed Him.** When He came to the place, He said to the "Pray that you may not enter into temptation." ...When He rose up from prayer, and had come to Him disciples, he found them sleeping from sorrow.*
Luke 22:39,40&45

————

Then Jesus came with them to a place called Gethsemane, and said to the disciples, "Sit here while I go and pray over there." ...Then He came to the disciples and found them sleeping, and said to Peter, "What? Could you not watch with Me one hour?"
Matthew 26:36&40

Though the disciples were with Him they were not in sync with Him. Granted, they were crippled by the fact that they did not yet have the Holy Spirit, but the point is you see Jesus imploring with them three times to pray and keep watch and be of one mind and heart with what was going on.

Let this mind be in you which was also in Christ Jesus.
Phil. 2:5

The word "mind" in this verse is "phroneo" in the Greek, and it encompasses the idea of the exercising of your thoughts and the desires of your heart. In some versions, it is interpreted into the word "attitude." Just as God implores us to not just follow, but be of the same attitude with Him, so we must do the same with our disciples.

When I discipline my kids I don't want them to just imitate me when I correct them or to just do what I tell them because they HAVE to. The goal is for them to see their sin and disobedience the way I do because I see like God sees it. This is true of discipleship. Our goal should not be to get our disciples to simply do what we do, but to think like we think, BECAUSE WE HAVE LEARNED TO THINK LIKE GOD.

To Assist

Jesus was inviting the disciples to accompany as well as assist Him in His work.

And Jesus took the loaves, and when He had given thanks He distributed them to the disciples, and the disciples to those sitting down; and likewise the fish, as much as they wanted.
John 6:11

———

...He blessed and broke and gave the loaves to the disciples; and the disciples gave to the multitudes.
Matthew 14:19b

In the feeding of the multitude, the disciples aren't just in attendance, but they are invited in on the distribution of the miraculous provision. They assist Jesus in feeding the multitude. This is a huge component in discipleship...that we allow our disciples to assist us, and not just because we need the help. Jesus didn't need their help, but He invited them in for the purpose of them being a part of what He was doing and what He was all about.

Although He gives them instructions on how to accomplish the task in an orderly fashion, ultimately He lets them do it. This can be a challenge for those of us who are a bit of control freaks. We tend not to invite others in either because we don't need their help, and/or we want to make sure it is done "right" AKA, our way. But, this is not the case with Jesus. Remember, He has a plan here, and it is not just to feed the multitude, but also to raise up His disciples.

So He seizes this opportunity to challenge them to step into the position and abilities He has had in mind for them from the beginning. Consider the fullness of all the disciples learned in just this one act and how much of that might have gotten lost if they were simply observing and not assisting. After all, they were handed five loaves and two fish, and it wasn't until they began to operate obediently on faith that the measly meal turned into a feast with leftovers!

The "One-Two Punch"

Notice that it was as the disciples assisted Jesus that they stepped into who He created them to be. I believe Jesus was intentional to set up those opportunities for them to succeed in their new roles. We will learn as we look at more examples of how Jesus discipled that there is always what I call the "one-two punch." The one-two punch is when there is a combination of going and meeting someone where they are, pulling them in through relationship, but then challenging them to shoot forth into who they are created to be.

This happens through opportunity; a set up to step up. We do this because our goal is to help them step into the fullness of who they are in Christ. Jesus never saw someone in accordance to who they were in the world, but He saw who they were in the Spirit. He sees who they are created to be and the purpose they are designed to fulfill. I love that Jesus was all about speaking a reputation INTO His disciples and then setting up opportunities for them to demonstrate their potential. Think about it, while the world was calling Simon, "Simon," Jesus was calling him "Peter."

Blessed are you, Simon Bar-Jonah, for flesh and blood has not revealed this to you but My Father who is in heaven. And I say to you that you are Peter, and on this rock I will build My church, and the gates of Hades shall not prevail against it. And I will give you the keys of the kingdom of heaven and whatever you bind on earth will be bound in heaven, and whatever you loosed on earth will be loosed in heaven.
Matthew 16:17-19

This is quite the reputation. Poor Simon had simply responded to the question, "

But who do you say that I am?" (Matthew 16:15) And next thing you know, Jesus is speaking "craziness" over him! But this is so important in discipleship. We must look at our disciples and see what God sees and then challenge them with opportunities to step up. This happens as we invite them not to just "follow us" or accompany but assist us as well.

I am not sure how Peter took this, but I know that there have been times when someone has spoken something over me that has caused me to look over my shoulder to see if they are talking to someone behind me. And although their words were so "big" and there was an element of fear and anxiety, I felt a rising up within me. In other words, my soul realm was a bit freaked, but my Spirit was quickened and bore witness, responding with a resounding, "Yes and amen!"

Kate has spent many years challenging me to step into who I am by giving me practical directives. I spoke of her combination of speaking grace and truth earlier and this is the same concept. There's a little love tap to get my attention, with a punch to compel me forward. There is a gentle, friendly invitation that comes through relationship, with a shove to challenge an execution. I cannot tell you how important this concept is in discipleship.

We see it in sports and the way a coach moves a mediocre player into a star on the court. The coach has an eye to recognize talent and invites the player to come and learn, but the coach's goal is to shoot that player into his full potential. This comes as the coach offers up opportunities for the player to step up on the playing field. The coach typically expects more of the player than the player thinks they are capable of, but the coach knows the potential of the player. The ultimate goal is to get the player to know his fullness as well.

God is like that with us. He looks at us and says, "You're not Abram the barren, but you are Abraham, the father of many…you're not Mary the lowly virgin, but you are Mary the highly favored, you're not Saul the blasphemer and persecutor, but you are Paul the missionary…" You see, Jesus was demonstrating the heart of God in the way He raised up His disciples and so should we!

Let's examine the main points of the one-two punch a little more closely through examples in the Scriptures.

Meet Your Disciple Where They Are

But He needed to go through Samaria. So He came to a city of Samaria which is called Sychar, near the plot of ground that Jacob gave to his son Joseph. Now Jacob's well was there. Jesus therefore, being wearied from His journey, sat thus by the well. It was about the sixth hour. A woman of Samaria came to draw water. Jesus said to her, "Give Me a drink."
John 4:4-7

Jesus went to where the woman was via the prompting of the Spirit, mind you. This is important, because often our soul realm, meaning our feelings, our thoughts or even our will or personal desires will try to get us to engage with someone that the Lord is not leading us to. This is not best. When we go to meet someone where they are, we must be walking in accordance to the Spirit and not the flesh, otherwise we will get our self in the way of the assignment at hand.

Jesus' example to us in this passage demonstrates that He is willing to go out of His way and lay down His own agenda and needs at that moment to connect with this woman. We also see that He goes to where no one else would go at that particular time of the day and He does what no one else would.

I think it is interesting to note that Jesus meets the

woman in Sychar, which in the Greek means, "drunken."
Now, we can interpret this in many ways, but the point is
He does NOT meet her in the holy temple or in the church.
Instead, He meets her where she is in HER environment. In
many ways, the "well" in this passage represents idolatry
meaning the place where she went to "be filled" day after
day.

I think it is also significant that she went at a time when
she knew no one else would be there, at high noon. This
was when the sun was hottest and therefore in that culture
the common time to go to the well was in the mornings or
evenings, yet there she was going "in secret" to get her fill.
The point is that often we sit in our "holy place," both
literally and metaphorically, and throw out our invites
instead of going out, meeting people where they are, and
getting them. We have to be willing to go into the world to
make disciples, not for the purpose of hanging out with
them, but for the purpose of connecting to them and WITH
them.

Jesus found His disciples in their environment; fishing,
tax collecting, sitting under the fig tree, etc. He did NOT
find them in the temple. We must be willing to connect
with people in their environment or even in their sin in
order to pull them into the kingdom. This does NOT mean
we should LOOK like the world or do what they are doing.
In fact, the Word is clear that we should be set apart from
the world, but let's not misinterpret that into thinking we
can't go to where they are to love them INTO the Kingdom.

Even after the resurrection, we find Jesus going to where

His people are. We see Him showing up for breakfast by the sea with the disciples in the midst of their failure and despair. We see Him meeting Thomas in the midst of his doubt. We see Him on the road to Emmaus in the midst of the disciples' fear. We find Him in the upper room where the disciples are hiding in the midst of their fear.

He FOUND them...He went to where they were physically and connected with their hearts for the purpose of instilling hope and bringing them back to their positions as disciples! What a beautiful example shown to us by Jesus Himself of connecting with others right where they are.

Connect With Them and Develop a Relationship

*"He appointed twelve, **that they might be with Him**, and that He might send them out to preach, and to have authority to cast out the demons"*
Mark 3:14, 15

Notice that Jesus' relationship with His disciples **preceded** His assignment to them. Relationship is such a huge concept in discipleship. I have mentioned several times the loss of one-on-one relationship in our culture. With all the technologies we have out there, face-to-face interaction has become something of the past. We don't even talk to a human for customer service much anymore. We must be intentional to build a relationship with those we are called to disciple. This is the beauty of the "follow me" concept. When you do as Jesus did, relationships organically develop...and remember, that is what we are after, organic discipleship.

Once we meet our disciple where they are, we must invite them to come be with us where we are. We want to spend time with them and develop a relationship with them for the purpose of gaining trust and respect. I think that we often think that discipling someone means that we go around speaking Truths, giving unsolicited advice, and telling people what to do. THIS IS NOT DISCIPLESHIP! In fact, this is nothing but offensive and a turn off to today's generation.

We must recognize the importance of earning the right in their lives to speak truth into them. This is done through relationship. Jesus met people where they were and then connected with them. He spent time with His disciples and developed a relationship with them. I think that we, in our pride, think that discipleship means letting our disciples know how much knowledge we have. But remember the old adage, "People don't care how much you know until they know how much you care." The Word says, "Knowledge puffs up, but love builds up."

In the Welcome Home Ministry, we recognize that when the ladies first move in, they have some major trust issues. And although we technically have the right to tell them what to do and how to do it, the Lord has taught us that there is wisdom in loving them right where they are first. We are sensitive and intentional to love them well and EARN their trust. The things that these ladies have been through leave them on their guard, and ultimately, we want them to feel safe…not just practically, but emotionally.

If we were to just start "arm twisting" them, there would be no long-term result. Ultimately, it is the love that we show them and through relationship that they are transformed from the inside out. The goal is not for them to change because they have to but because they WANT to. This only happens as we build into their lives through relationship.

Relationship requires time…and patience, A LOT of it! But if you utilize the follow me concept, it is much simpler. Having 6 children and a full-time ministry means a whole lot of busyness in my life, so my disciples have learned to just come with me where I go. And "along the road," we talk as we go and I explain things to them; let them in on what I am thinking and what I am doing and why I am doing it.

I do a whole lot of counseling and praying in the car as we are going from one place to the next. One of my favorite things is to take a disciple along with me when I travel. This is when they get to see my daily habits 24/7, when I pray, how I pray, what I am reading in Scripture and how the Word is speaking to me. This is raw, organic…and easy!!

We can't skip the relationship portion of discipleship. It simply won't work. I personally believe that Jesus spent more time alone with His disciples than anything else. He understood that He would ultimately reach the masses by reaching individuals.

One at a time, each of us can disciple and together we will collectively raise up an army of disciples, not just converts. We need to recognize the power of one and be content to start with that.

The Punch to Challenge

This is the part of the "One-two punch" that I love! If you knew me, you would know why I said that. I am a Truth teller, I love to be challenged, and I love to challenge others. After you have met your disciple where they are and your relationship is on its way, it is important that you challenge your disciple for the purpose of pushing them forward. We want them to step into who they REALLY are in Christ.

We must discern the heart and personality of our disciple to know how much challenge they can take. I know that because I am prophetic I often lack in tenderness and mercy. God has gifted me to see so clearly the potential of others that I tend to get irritated when they falter in faintheartedness or despair, or when they sit stuck in their sin/trial/circumstance. I say this to share that it is important that you speak the Truth in love and that your challenge to them is done for the purpose of setting them up to succeed.

Your disciple must know that you are FOR them, not against them. They need to know that you are on their side with God AGAINST their challenges and oppositions.

The ladies in our Home get to feel this every month

when we evaluate their progress and set new 30-day goals. Ultimately, they set their own goals, but we encourage them each month to progressively intensify those goals. We challenge them in every aspect of their lives, Spirit, soul and body and they typically very willingly agree because they know that we are FOR them and that we want to see them succeed.

This is ONLY established after building a relationship through love. I would love to tell you that these ladies come into the Home so desperate that they immediately do everything we ask or recommend, and they do, for about the first 30 days. But after the "honeymoon phase" is over, most of them begin to test the waters and they get a bit fussy with us, if not downright disrespectful and rebellious. They challenge the rules, they fall short on their goals, and they do things their own way instead of heeding our advice. I am telling you that with almost every single one, we have seen this pattern. I am convinced that this is because they are testing our love for them.

I don't think this is a conscious thought, but there is something in them that fears success and is comfortable in their captivity of failure, rejection and lack. It sounds strange, but it is no different than the Israelites who begged to go back to Egypt and feared entering into the promise land...they too tested the waters and fussed about Moses who was simply trying to help them. Ultimately, Moses himself took up for the Israelites and pleaded for them, even to God Himself. He understood the freedom that was due them, and he challenged them to keep moving forward, even when they had sinned. He was with them in their wilderness, and he loved them in their wilderness.

There are many discipleship programs out there, but Jesus Himself provides some excellent examples for us through the "follow me" concept and the "one-two punch." We would do well to look more closely at these concepts in the gospels and apply them to our own lives in understanding discipleship. This is what we try to imitate: discipleship by coming alongside others in their wandering and loving them in the midst of it. Reaching out to them and connecting with them through relationship, inviting them to follow us and then challenging them to move forward and execute victoriously.

CHAPTER 5
THE DISCIPLESHIP PROCESS IN THE SCRIPTURES

WHEN I GO into a church or organization to teach on discipleship or do the Discipleship Conference, I ask those who will be attending to read Mark chapters 3, 4, 5 & 6 before I come. I encourage them to watch for the relationship between Jesus and His disciples and to consider the intentionality of Jesus with His disciples and to details of what the disciples were doing in the midst of it all. I love the succession of these chapters, because you can see a clear example of some of the concepts we have discussed already with regard to discipleship.

Mark 3 – The Call to Follow

The process starts in Mark 3 where Jesus calls His disciples. This goes back to the "follow me" concept. I would be remiss if I did not point out "the call" as the beginning of the progression we are about to look at. "The call" is the starting place of the discipleship relationship. People often ask if Kate pursued me or I pursued her. In our case, I pursued her, but we see both in the Scriptures. Sometimes Jesus calls His disciples, but others find Him. But either way, there is clearly commitment that is made in the relationship.

When I know that God has "assigned" a particular person as a disciple to me, there is typically an intentional commitment that I make to pour into that person. I tend to discuss this with my husband and am sure to "count the cost." The reverse is true as well. While Kate has been my foundational mentor for 18 years, there are others whom the Lord has brought for particular areas of my life for particular seasons. When I sense that He has brought that person for me to "sit under," there is a commitment that I make to receive from that person.

I prioritize time and activities that involve that person, because I know that it is part of God's plan in growing me, and I WANT that. I welcome that person into my life, and I try to accompany that person in their work as much as possible.

Mark 4 – Receiving Information

There is typically a "receiving of information" part in every teaching process. In Mark chapter 4 we see Jesus demonstrating this process of giving information.

And again He began to teach by the sea. And a great multitude was gathered to Him, so that He got into a boat and sat in it on the sea; and the whole multitude was on the land facing the sea. Then He taught them many things by parables, and said to them in His teaching.
Mark 4:1&2

Now remember, we want to pay attention to where the disciples were and what their role was in all of this. Jesus was intentional, and everything He did included raising up His disciples; therefore, we must note that the disciples weren't simply there...they were WITH HIM. So they too were receiving from the teaching of various parables that are given in Mark 4. This was the "lecture" portion of learning like when we attend class and sit in front of the professor and soak up information and glean from the wisdom of those who clearly know more than we do.

In the parables, Jesus wasn't just giving them valuable information about the Kingdom of God, but He was also connecting it to things that they would be able to relate to. In other words, He wasn't just presenting information; He was presenting it in a way that was relevant to their world. Seeds, farmers, lamps, crops, trees, herbs, these were things that their brains could connect with because they were part of their everyday life.

We all would agree that the "good" professors or teachers are the ones that can present their information in a way that we can connect and understand it. This is an important part of discipleship, times when we sit one on one with our disciple and just teach them, explain things, and give them information and present it in a way that is relevant to them personally.

I think we as a body of believers do a great job giving and getting information through times like when we sit in front of a pastor in church, or with a mentor, or an elder, or a Sunday School teacher and simply receive information from them.

Just like teachers or professors, the "good" pastors or teachers are the ones that we can connect with because they present the information in a way that applies to us personally. They present information in a way that is relevant to today's culture and those we are ministering to. I cannot tell you how many times the ladies in our Home ask us what the message in church was about or how it relates to their daily challenges.

People in general often ask, what does that message have to do with my anger, or my depression, or my marriage, or my headaches, or my...fill in the blank? Although giving information is a very valuable part of discipleship, it must be relevant or it will go in one ear and out the other. Church messages are often being completely dismissed, because they are not relevant.

The gospel message is often dismissed, because we don't present the daily relevance of Jesus to everyday life. So while the information portion of discipleship is important, we need to make sure our disciples can connect the information to their own life...and we must not stop at just giving information.

Mark 5 – See One, The Demonstration

Let's go back to a concept I spoke of earlier called "See one, do one, teach one." This is a concept that much of our world has adopted in order to bring another person "into" a trade. Look at how you can see Jesus utilize this same concept to disciple His followers.

The "see one" portion can only take place if we are giving our disciples something to see. This means raising disciples requires us to demonstrate. Jesus did not just speak the Word, He WAS the Word.

And the Word became flesh and dwelt among us, and we beheld His glory...
John 1:14.

The Word was "fleshed out" in the person of Jesus Christ...it was MANIFEST in human form so that all could SEE the demonstration of the Word of God.

The Word was not just delivered verbally, but it was demonstrated, it was activated through movement, and was made flesh through Him. This is our goal as well, not that we would have knowledge of the Word, but that we would live the Word. We want the Word of God to be fleshed out in our lives...the Word of God made flesh IN us! This comes much easier when we can see it demonstrated through another, more specifically through a mentor.

There were several times when Kate would give me instruction on how to discipline my children, but because I was so often WITH her, I got to see her discipline her own children. This was far more effective than just being told. We follow the same model with the ladies in our Home. There are times when they meet with us and learn Biblical principles about child training, or they are required to attend workshops in regard.

But we also OFTEN go into the Home and just hang out in order to take advantage of opportunities to demonstrate for them as things arise with the children. We also find role-play very effective. This is where two of us will role-play, one being mom, the other being child. We are intentional to point out as we demonstrate every detail from body language, body positioning, and affection during discipline, to verbiage, tone, and attitude. This takes time and requires us to be available often impromptu, but it is extremely relevant to their situation, because IT IS their situation.

We see the same with Jesus in Mark 5. In this one chapter, Jesus delivers a demon-possessed man, He heals the woman with the issue of blood, and He raised Jairus's daughter from the dead. A deliverance, a healing, and a resurrection…all on the heels of the ministry of the Word.

What we see here is the full gospel manifested and displayed through the person of Jesus Christ. But, let's remember that though the man was delivered, the woman was healed, and the daughter was resurrected, Jesus was also intentionally teaching His disciples through those miracles. I am certainly NOT downplaying the miracles, but I AM "up-playing" the discipleship process that took place through those miracles.

Think about all the disciples learned through Jesus' demonstrative works. Not just the deliverance, but how He responded and interacted with the demon possessed man who was uncontrollable and "cast off" by the world, or the way He stopped and took note despite the crowd to acknowledge the woman.

And Jesus, immediately knowing in Himself that power had gone out of Him, turned around in the crowd and said, "Who touched My clothes?" But His disciples said to Him, "You see the multitude thronging You, and You say, 'Who touched Me?'"
Mark 5:30-31

I love these verses because amid all that is going on, we see that there is interaction taking place between Jesus and His disciples. I find it interesting and worth noting that even in the chaos of this crowd that was "thronging" about Him, the disciples felt a freedom to ask Him a question. There is part of me that chuckles at the audacity of the disciples questioning the Lord, especially in front of people, but there is a bigger part of me that finds it refreshing and liberating. This shows me that they had developed enough of a relationship with Him that they could approach Him boldly anytime and anyplace.

Now look at the intentional "placement" of the disciples in the resurrection of Jairus's daughter.

*And He permitted no one to follow Him except Peter, James, and John the brother of James...HE took the father and the mother of the child, **and those who were with Him,** and entered where the child was lying.*
Mark 5:37

Here we see that Jesus has three of His disciples, who He considers His "inner circle," come in to witness the miracle of bringing life to the dead. There is an important lesson here, and we must not pass this by. Jesus is very intentional in all that He does, so we know that He has granted them access for a purpose, and I am pretty sure it is NOT because he needs their help to raise Jairus's daughter from the dead. After all, He is God incarnate!

I believe it is because He takes seriously the idea of letting them accompany Him and see Him function, even behind closed doors. This was an intimate moment with this family, yet Jesus does not miss the opportunity for demonstration to His disciples.

A huge part of Crazy8 Ministries is our intern and apprenticeship programs. This is where we allow younger or less seasoned believers to come and "hang out" around the Grounds. We bring them into our counseling rooms and prayer rooms (with the client's consent) as much as possible. We give them duties around the office and teach them how we need it done and why. We take them into the Home with us to observe how we interact with the ladies and their children and then after we let them in on why we do what we do, or why we handle things the way we did. We also take them with us wherever we go.

I do a lot within our community, which requires me to attend a lot of public events as well as private meetings. Most of the people that I sit on boards with are very accustomed to the fact that I am almost never unaccompanied by someone.

Much like Jesus did, I don't just allow them to accompany me to public events, but also to private meetings. This is extremely effective in raising someone up. It affords them to see me in all different settings and function in many different roles. They see me function not just as the Founder of Crazy8, but as secretary, or "worker bee," or just as a quiet member. It is important that they not just HEAR me speak to them about serving others, but they get to see it demonstrated. There are many times that I am not the one "in charge" and they need to see that and how I function in those roles.

Elisha washed the hands of Elijah before he got the double portion, and no matter where we are we need to remember the importance of serving and being Elisha. I want my disciples to learn that from me, but more importantly to see it IN me. This is why our willingness to take them with us wherever we go is so important…it gives them the opportunity to "See one."

Mark 6 – Do One, The Practice

Discipleship is most effectively taught by demonstration

and most effectively learned through practice. This means actually DOING what you have just learned. Consider with me how a person becomes skilled at a sport or playing an instrument. There is certainly a time of learning information, or watching a demonstration, but ultimately, practice MUST come into play.

My husband was a basketball coach for years, and if his practices had only consisted of him verbally instructing his players on plays, they would never be able to execute those plays. But instead there was instruction, demonstration, and then practice. So, there was a time of watching game tapes or Brad demonstrating after he would give verbal instructions, but then they would go out onto the court and practice it!

This is the "Do one" portion that is so important in teaching our disciples how to execute information and knowledge. This goes back to the challenge portion of the one-two punch where we afford opportunities to practice while we are with them. I personally assign my disciples things to do daily to practice executing Truths so that when they step into the game, the play is automatic. This includes all kinds of fun assignments from practicing healthy thinking to practicing praise to practicing praying out loud.

Many believers aren't comfortable praying out loud simply because they have never practiced it. It may sound corny, but why not practice praying over yourself daily while looking at yourself in the mirror?! Try it! You will find that you will be much more confident the next time you have the opportunity to pray out loud in front of people or with someone because you have been practicing it. Not to mention that there is power in speaking the Word, and you will no doubt become more confident because of it.

The point of practicing in anything you are learning is to bring you to a place of confidence and victory where you don't hesitate because you have a knowing and a confidence in your abilities because you have practiced so much. The disciples were afforded opportunities to practice ministering while Jesus was still here on earth, whether it was in His presence or when they were sent to minister.

There are many examples where we see Him inviting them in to be a part of the manifestations of miracles and challenging them to lunge into who they were to become. But, we also see Him sending them out to function without Him. Keep in mind that we actually have "one up" on the disciples, because we are indwelt and empowered by the Holy Spirit no matter where we go.

And He called the twelve to Himself, and began to send them out two by two, and gave them power over unclean spirits. ...So they went out and preached that people should repent. And they cast out many demons, and anointed with oil many who were sick, and healed them.
Mark 6:7, 12&13.

Jesus brought His disciples in and then sent them out. And, they imitated what He had been demonstrating. They were preaching, delivering, and healing. Exactly what we see Jesus doing in Mark 4 and 5! Do you see this progression? This is a beautiful picture of how we should be discipling our own.

I love that He sent His disciples out. Sending our disciples out and affording them the opportunity to do what they have been observing and practicing is very effective in raising them up. This not only lets our disciples know that we think they have what it takes, but it also lets them know that they have what it takes. It is one thing for them to practice a "skill" or Truth in a controlled environment, it is another to send them out and let them go.

I try to take some of our interns, which we affectionately call "younglings," with us to as many conferences as possible. I try to give them specific assignments that will require them to take ownership of a particular portion of the conference. I typically know where one of them is and what their strengths and weaknesses are, but I am always looking to stretch them through opportunity.

I recently gave them an assignment of putting together a photo show summarizing the past year of the ministry. I gave them no instructions other than I wanted it to capture the year and all the arms of the ministry, and I wanted it no longer than 3 minutes. They had a limited time frame to accomplish this, and I was preparing for my message. When they were finished they asked if I wanted to see it and I said no.

I think they were shocked because I typically preview everything, but this group of girls needed this boost of confidence. They had done several media projects for me with me sitting next to them walking them through it, so I trust their ability and they know what I like. In other words, they had practiced this skill and were ready to step out! It was great for them, and they did a great job!

After there has been much practice and doing, it is time to move into the next phase, which is turning around, and teaching.

Teach One

Of course the goal here is for us to bring our disciples to a place of raising up more disciples. I often ask in our conferences, "When was the last time you discipled someone to the place where they are raising up other disciples?" Unfortunately, there are typically almost no hands that go up. Jesus wasn't raising up disciples to just have a fabulous relationship with God, and He wasn't raising up disciples to just to get others converted into Christianity. He was raising up disciples for the purpose of raising up more disciples and multiplying the Kingdom. This is an example of network marketing at its finest. Jesus raised up His 12, and then immediately in Acts, we see the disciples multiplying the Kingdom.

But Peter, standing up with the eleven, raised his voice and said to them, "Men of Judea and all who dwell in Jerusalem, let this be known to you, and heed my words..."
Acts 2:14

Then those who gladly received his word were baptized; and that day about three thousand souls were added to them. And they continued steadfastly in the apostles' doctrine and fellowship, in the breaking of bread, and in prayers.
Acts 2:41&42

———

*Now all who believed **were together**, and had all things in common…So continuing daily with one accord in the temple, and breaking bread from house to house, they ate their food with gladness and simplicity of heart, praising God and having favor with all the people. And the Lord added to the church daily those who were being saved.*
Acts 2:44, 46&47

Don't just look at the multiplication of converts here, but notice that they CONTINUED STEADFASTLY in all the apostles were doing. I think given the next portions of Scripture, it is fair to assume that they brought these converts IN to be a part of their DAILY living for the purpose of discipling them and raising up more disciples. In all that we have learned, I would say there was some organic discipleship starting to unfold here. So, we don't just see the disciples doing what Jesus did, but they are raising up more disciples by bringing them in and discipling them.

We love to afford our interns opportunities to teach others. We do a lot of "big sister/big brother" stuff with our younger clients and with our kiddos in the shelter. We recognize that kids (as well as adults) long for relationship and time. As counselors, we aren't always able to just "hang out" or play with the kids, so we supplement our counseling times with a "big sister or brother."

This not only benefits the kids, but the interns learn a lot as well. We see a lot of growth on both ends through this process, and frankly it is our way of working smarter and not harder as counselors. It is a win-win.

What a beautiful progression we see in the Scriptures on how to make disciples. I pray that you are beginning to recognize how discipleship is a process that moves people to a place of execution, that we must follow Jesus' example to us when discipling others and move them from just knowing the Word to being the Word fleshed out.

CHAPTER 6
CULTURAL BAPTISM

WHEN JESUS WAS HERE on earth, He completely
redefined the "religious" culture of the day. It was totally
different than what they currently knew of religion for
several reasons. But, the point is that by inviting the
disciples to "follow Him," He wanted to submerge them
into His life and this new culture. This is what I call cultural
baptism. I have heard it called discipleship by immersion
as well. Call it what you want, but it is the idea of
completely submerging someone in a particular culture.
This means bringing people into your environment so they
can just organically begin to "pick things up."

Whether we like it or not, we are all being discipled and
so are our children. The question is who or what is
discipling us? Consider the influence that music, media,
peers, education systems, politics, or even churches have on
people. When we are exposed daily to a certain way of

thinking, or behavior, or language, or belief system etc., we naturally begin to pick up those same things. If you or I were to fly to another country for a year, we would naturally begin to pick up on their language, the style of dress, their cultural practices, their taste in food, and so on.

This is a no brainer. We would be baptized or immersed into their culture, and it would be organic. We see this concept in the Acts where those who were converted were brought into the daily practices of the disciples. They fellowshipped together, had things in common, ate together, worshipped together, etc. The disciples of Jesus did for the new converts what Jesus had done with them first.

The age-old concept of apprenticeship was that a young boy between the ages of 10-15 would go to reside with his "master" for sometimes up to seven years. The apprentice received training, along with housing and food in exchange for his work and assistance to the "master." They were completely submerged into the "master's" life and culture. It was actually from this concept of apprenticeship that the government began to formalize the process and developed what we now know as universities and colleges. It is fun to note that most Master's Degrees require a season of interning within the field that is being studied.

This is one of the biggest reasons why Brad and I have opened up our home to my disciples, not just for them to come hang out, but for them to actually live with us. Our girls have stayed with us anywhere from three months to a year. Of course there is much prayer that goes into this, but we love it! I understand that this is not for everyone, but for us it has proven to be a blessing.

They get to experience and see everything about us and the way we function. They learn how to clean, how to discipline, how to communicate, how to manage a family of eight, and much more. They also get to see me all the time, which honestly has challenged and refined me personally. Trust me, these girls have gotten to see my "real, raw" times, but even in that, there is a gleaning process. The perk is that they are a real help to me as well in that they help with the chores, errands, rides, etc.

That is the "assistance" part of the follow me concept we have looked at several times. I have had the honor of watching some of these girls get married and move into their own homes, and they practice a lot of the same things that we do, because they were discipled by the culture of our home.

We have set Crazy8 up with the same concept in mind, in many regards. Staff and volunteers typically all start out by just "hanging" out or being around us. We encourage them to just come and be present in the office and observe or converse with other staff as much as possible. I mentioned earlier that we let our apprentices and interns follow us and hang out. That is the same concept being practiced here…it is a cultural baptism. And, in regard to the ladies and children in our Home, this concept is very important to the effectiveness of Crazy8.

We have intentionally positioned the Home right next to our offices for the purpose of discipling them by immersion. We have had several people ask why I don't accumulate homes throughout our community so that I can house more women. In fact, I have had people offer me homes, but the reality is it would not work. We are not interested in just housing these ladies, but rather completely restoring every aspect of their lives.

This means we must be in contact with them daily, but more importantly they must be in contact with us. So while the Welcome Home Admin Team spend a lot of time IN the Home, the ladies spend a lot of time IN the office. We encourage them to come hang out with us whenever they want. We bring them in to answer the phones or invite them along with us to conferences or just be around us. Organically, we see changes. They begin to pick up on how we instruct our children around the Grounds (we often have our own kids there), or the way we interact with one another, or the way we respond in particular situations. I am convinced that this probably has more effect than we even know.

I will never forget one of the first times one of the ladies gave a public testimony of the help she was receiving at Crazy8. She talked a little bit about the practical help that we were able to be to her, but, more than anything, I remember her beginning to cry as she explained that she had been changed just by the atmosphere of love.

She expressed that it wasn't just the love we showed to her, but that she was amazed by the love we had for each other too. Through tears, she tried to express how strange that was for her to experience this, because she had never known love like that. She ended by saying that the practical things we did daily were a huge help to her, but it was the culture of love that was transforming her. There was not a dry eye in the room. It absolutely confirmed to me that it was working.

This is one of the reasons why the program is 18-24 months. It takes a lot of time to deprogram and reprogram our residents. Most of these ladies have spent years living in survival mode, and there is MUCH that needs to be addressed and worked on. They are required to meet with a counselor once a week, and they meet with their caseworker regularly as well. Those are the times when they sit down and receive information.

They are given spiritual, Biblical, and practical assignments weekly to practice new thinking, new habits, new attitudes, and frankly to just move them forward in life. They are given things to practice regularly and must attend a church weekly as well. But in conjunction with all of this, they are simply baptized into our culture because they live there and are exposed to us daily. I believe that it truly is the atmosphere of love that the Lord has established on our Grounds that produces the supernatural changes. No man or program can do that, only the love of God can! This is why we have an open-door policy; the ladies know that they are welcome in the office.

A lot of people mention that our office "feels" good. Even people who are not that familiar with God have said things like, "I just love coming here and could just sit in the waiting room all day." Others have said things like, "I don't need to see a counselor because as soon as I walk in, a peace falls upon me." I promise you, I am not making this up. This is obviously only because of His Presence on the Grounds and in the office.

But God has taught us to stir up the anointing by continual praise and worship in all that we do. We do not engage in negativity, nor do we tolerate complaining and fussing. It spoils the anointing. But instead, He has taught us the power of His love and the peace that accompanies those set on His love. We are intentional to practice expressing and showing love toward Him and each other publicly and verbally throughout the day. We also spend much time in prayer and prayer walking. Guess what?

People sense a difference, and they are affected by the culture that has been set up and they find themselves wanting to hang out more and more.

I try to be intentional to position myself in places where I will grow in my relationship with the Lord. I realize that I will pick up that which I am immersed in, so I want to be wise and remember that I am responsible for all that I am exposed to as well as what I am exposing others to. We must not forget the concept of cultural baptism and the power that it has, both for the good and the bad.

CHAPTER 7
BEING A TIMOTHY FIRST

WHEN EITHER WE train on discipleship or do a discipleship conference, we often ask people to consider whether or not they consider themselves a Paul, a Timothy or a Barnabas. Of course, I realize that in different settings we may fall into a different category, and that is good. We should all have a Paul, a Timothy and a Barnabas in our lives, and we should all at some points be a Paul, a Timothy and a Barnabas.

A Paul is one who, like Paul, raised up others and made disciples, particularly Timothy. He spoke into the lives of others and carried a spiritual rank in their lives. We are "Pauls" to our children and to those whom we pour into. The whole purpose of this book is to teach us what it means to BE a Paul and to raise up our "Timothys" into "Pauls."

A Barnabas on the other hand is an encourager. Those

are the people in our lives with whom we have a camaraderie, and we come along side of each other on the "same plane," if you will.

As iron sharpens iron, so a man sharpens the countenance of his friend.
Proverbs 27:17

This verse captures the essence of those "Barnabas" relationships in our lives well. These are vital and beautiful, and frankly the most common relationships.

That brings us to Timothy and what that means. What does it mean to be a Timothy? I would be remiss if we skipped over the importance of being a Timothy and only talked about being a Paul. Being a Timothy is what should ultimately and organically launch us into the Paul position. So let's plunge deeper into the Timothy concept.

Selling a Product

We typically say that a product sells itself, but I disagree, people sell products. You don't see a pair of jeans on a commercial; you see them on a person, typically one who looks AMAZING in the jeans. When someone is selling something, they typically know all about that product and they are typically in love with that product. They believe in it. I love the Mary Kay Foundation and our local Mary Kay chapter is very supportive of Crazy8, which makes me love them more.

But one of the things that I have noticed is that these ladies are passionate about their product, and they know it inside and out. Honestly, they can be a bit obnoxious in their continual talk of all the latest products and hottest colors, but one thing I know is that they are proud to represent Mary Kay.

Mary Kay doesn't sell itself, these ladies do. Personally it isn't the product itself but rather their belief in the product and love for the product that compelled me to first try it. And their continual belief and passion is what makes me "all in!"

When we go out into the community, it is so easy for me to talk about Crazy8 and what God is doing because I am passionate about it. I have had people say over and over things like, "All you need to do is get her in front of the people, and she will sell the ministry because of her passion and excitement." Or, "There is no question that you believe in what God is doing when you share about Crazy8."

This is not because I am a savvy talker or that I have all the right marketing skills, in fact, I have NO marketing training at all. But I DO know my product, and I believe in it and am passionate about it.

When my staff ask me to sit down and teach them a 45-second "elevator" speech, I simply ask them this question, "What in the world would make you quit your paying job to come work at Crazy8 full time for no pay?!" As they give me their answer, I quickly tell them, "That is YOUR elevator speech and that is what will sell Crazy8."

Here is my point, we can't sell something we don't

know and aren't passionate about. People won't buy into a product that the seller himself doesn't believe in. A Mary Kay consultant can talk to me all day about their makeup, but if she isn't wearing it, I am not likely to buy in. The fact that a Mary Kay consultant actually wears the products is what DEMONSTRATES that they love the product and believe in it.

So we can talk about Jesus all day long and say whatever we want, but unless they see evidence of Him on our face and in our life, why in the world would they buy in?

In the introduction of this book I asked this question, "How can we chemically create what should be happening organically within the Christian culture?" But, I want to ask another question to challenge us a step further. "Why isn't it organically happening?" If we truly understood the fullness of God and His love for us on a daily basis, wouldn't we just automatically be going and making disciples? Wouldn't it just be organic?

Knowing God

I fear that too often as believer's we know ABOUT God, but we don't KNOW God.

Now Jesus and His disciples went out to the towns of Caesarea Philippi; and on the road He asked His disciples, saying them, "Who do men say that I am?" So they answered, "John the Baptist; but some say, Elijah; and others, one of the prophets." He

said to them, "But who do you say that I am?" Peter answered and said to Him, "You are the Christ."
Mark 8:27-29

I love this passage of Scripture because I believe that Jesus was challenging the disciples to really assess how well they knew Him for themselves. Many times I ask clients to tell me who God or Jesus is to them, and, much like the disciples, they answer by telling what others say or have told them. I definitely get this a lot from students..."Well, my parents have told me this, or my Sunday school teacher says that, or my Pastor has always preached this..." But when asked the next question, "But what do YOU think, who is He to YOU?"

Most people get stumped and often grasp for an answer. Let's be honest, many of us know all about Jesus, but do we REALLY know Him? I have led many people to the Lord just because I have asked that question.

Often they think that just because they know about the work of the cross that they are saved, but, when you ask some key questions, you find that they have never really grasped it for themselves and personalized it. They know about the Gift, they see the Gift, and often even see the tag with their name on it, but the Gift remains under the tree all wrapped up. The point is that even after salvation, we often never know who God is and the fullness of our new life in Him.

...work out your own salvation with fear and trembling; for it is God who works in you both to will and to do for His good pleasure.
Philippians 2:12&13

The phrase "work out" in this verse in the Greek means to perform, accomplish, achieve, to bring about; to fashion or render fit for a thing. I love the definition "to fashion," because I think it grasps the idea of fashioning our salvation to fit our lives, meaning we wear our salvation in a way that it fits beautifully. We talk a lot about having a relationship with Christ, but I am interested in having fellowship with Christ. This requires us to fashion or to "put on" the Word of God humbly so that we wear it daily, and it fits us perfectly!

So what does that look like and how do we get there? Let's pretend you and I meet. Maybe you attend a conference that Crazy8 is putting on or one at which I am a speaker. We exchange words or perhaps even sit down and have lunch together; I tell you a bit about my life and you do likewise.

You hear tidbits about me as I speak, so by the end of the weekend, you have learned quite a bit about me. In fact, if someone mentioned my name you might even say, "I know her," but do you really KNOW me? The answer is no. If you and I wanted to really get to know one another, we would take it a step further.

We would probably exchange phone numbers, or set up a time to get together again, and from there we would perhaps chat on the phone or occasionally go to lunch. And the more we talked and spent time together, no doubt the more intimate our relationship would grow. There are many people that I know about, and many that I have relationships with, but those with whom I fellowship are much fewer.

But, in order for that fellowship to remain, I must be intentional to nurture that relationship. I must "fashion" that person to my life. This is the same in our walk with Jesus. We must be intentional to nurture our growth so that He is seen in WHO we are, not just what we say because we wear Him for every occasion.

So what does this have to do with discipleship? Everything! It must be our own fellowship with God that COMPELS us to nurture the same in those around us. My desire is not to guilt you into making disciples. I am convinced that if we were all intentional to BE discipled first, then we would automatically go and do the same. The last thing I want is for you to go out in the flesh and make disciples because that is what Christians are supposed to do. Please don't.

Come and See

*He appointed twelve, **that they might be with Him,** and that He might send them out…*
Mark 3:14

Remember, Jesus established fellowship with disciples

BEFORE HE sent them out. His relationship always preceded His assignment. I love in John chapter 1 when two disciples are following Jesus, and they ask to see where He is staying.

*Then Jesus turned, and seeing them following, said to them, "What do you seek?" They said to Him, "Rabbi, where are You staying?" He said to them, "Come and see." They came and saw where He was staying, **and remained with Him that day...**" John 1:38&39*

Notice that Jesus doesn't just tell them about where He is staying, but instead He invites them to commune with Him for the entire day. Can you imagine?! ...spending an entire day where Jesus stayed and sitting in His Presence soaking up all of who He is? Look at what came forth from that fellowship.

One of the two who heard John speak, and followed Him (Jesus), was Andrew, Simon Peter's brother. He first found his own brother Simon, and said to him, "We have found the Messiah" (which is translated, the Christ). And he brought him to Jesus..." John 1:40-42

The natural outcome of their time with Jesus is that they went and got others and brought them to Jesus as well. They were compelled by their own experience, and they wanted others to experience it too! Their communion with

Jesus Himself filled them with a passion to go and tell and bring others to His feet as well.

Let's connect this and make it relevant to us by asking this question, "What if we spent our days truly communing with Jesus and soaking up His Presence and falling in love with Him? Would we, too, automatically just be compelled to go and bring others to His throne with us?"

We see the same in the very next passage where Jesus finds Philip and invites Philip to follow Him. Philip, after following Him, then goes and tells Nathanial compelling him to "Come and See" (John 1:46.) Shouldn't the cry of our lives be, "Come and see!"

Yes, it should, but the problem is that we are not compelled, and we are not compelled because we are not sold on our product, Jesus Christ, and we aren't sold because we don't know our product well enough. This somewhat redefines the idea of being "sold out for Christ." Remember, I am not talking about knowing ABOUT Him, but rather knowing Him.

Recently, I traveled to Cincinnati to do some training and general ministry. I was doing a house meeting, and when the worship ended, the power of God literally fell on me as I began to speak and He wiped away any thoughts that I had intended for that night. I stood there in complete silence for about 30 seconds (which feels like forever when all eyes are one you), waiting on the Lord to tell me what He was wanting. He clearly led me to 2 Cor. 5:13 and told me to read through 2 Cor. 6:10. That was it...no fancy message, no persuasive words, no music…just the Word of God.

The Holy Spirit was so heavily upon me that I could barely stand upright or even see straight. It took me about 45 minutes to make it through the passage, and as I read, the Truth of what was being spoken was searing my own soul as well as those in the room. I wept like never before as I became very aware of the depths of His love for me as well as for everyone in the room.

The point of the entire message was that we are not convinced of His love for us. He was pleading with those in the room to be reconciled with His love and therefore be compelled by that reconciliation to go and minister that reconciliation. This is what I am talking about.

We must be convinced ourselves before we go and try to convince others. If we were really convinced, it would be automatic. Proclaiming the love of Christ should be the overflow of sharing in the life of Christ.

Consider the entire story of the woman at the well in John 4. It was the woman's fellowship with Jesus at the well that compelled her to go and evangelize to the town of Samaria.

*The woman then left her waterpot, went her way into the city, and said to the men, "**Come, see** a Man who told me all things that I ever did…*
John 4:28-29

Jesus did not instruct the woman to go and tell, He

didn't have to because she was so convinced of who He was and His love for her that she was compelled. Her own experience and the revelation of Truth in her life filled her with a desire to go and tell. The love that He bestowed upon her was so convincing that she could not help herself, she HAD to run and tell the world. Let's take a look at the rest of the passage and how you can see this same concept even further.

And many of the Samaritans of that city believed in Him because of the word of the woman who testified, "He told me all that I ever did." So when the Samaritans had come to Him, they urged Him to stay with them; and He stayed there two days. And many more believed because of His own word. Then they said to the woman, Now we believe, not because of what you said, for we ourselves have heard Him and we know that this is indeed the Christ, the Saviour of the world."
John 4:39-42

This is the shift that we need to come into. A shift from believing because of the words of others, to believing because we are absolutely convinced ourselves. But, it was because of their urgency to have their OWN experience and their OWN revelation that brought that shift. They wanted to see this man for themselves and so they invited Him to stay with them, and He did. And as they soaked up His Presence, they became convinced. Are you seeing a pattern here?

This is an incredible revelation for us all. If only we

would come to a place where we so desperately want to pursue Him and be discipled INTO our OWN fellowship, then we would be like the woman who just went and shared this love. It would be organic, people wouldn't be able to shut us up or stop us from loving people and speaking about who He is. What if Jesus and His love would ooze from our lives so much that instead of us running to people they would be running to us and begging us to share what it is that we have that they are missing out on? That is how it was with Kate. I wanted what she had! And I needed her to take me there…I had to BE a Timothy and yield myself to discipleship first.

Being Teachable

And He spoke a parable to them, "Can the blind lead the blind? Will they not both fall into the ditch?" A disciple is not above his teacher, but everyone who is perfectly trained will be like his teacher."
Luke 6:39-40

It is so important that we stay in the humble state of being taught, lest we be found trying to lead others blindly. We often do a demonstration during the Discipleship Conference where we blindfold both a Paul and a Timothy and try to watch the Paul lead their disciple through an obstacle course. Obviously, it doesn't work. But then we take the blindfold off the Paul and give them just a generic list of directives to verbally (without looking at the course) try to talk the Timothy through the course.

That doesn't work either, just like a generic program or step-by-step manual that is written to instruct us how to disciple people typically doesn't work. Ultimately, we want the Paul to go the course first and then move alongside the disciple as they, still blindfolded, go through the course themselves. This is a great demonstration of discipling someone through their OWN course of life. We will talk later about discipling someone to be them and not you or anyone else. We aren't raising robots, we are raising people, and we don't want to conform them.

The point is that we can't lead the blind when we are blind ourselves. I can't teach someone to pray, when I haven't figured it out yet myself; or how to train their children, when mine are out of control. Now, does this mean we have to wait until we are perfect? No, but we do want to know what we are selling. And beyond that, we must be actively growing in our pursuit of Him. I personally do not think it would be right for me to impress upon others the importance of being a Timothy if I am not one myself.

The word "blind" in the verse above includes the idea of being blind with pride and conceit. Pride and conceit will keep you from seeking guidance and being teachable. There is nothing more frustrating than a disciple who says they want to be discipled but then responds with, "I know," or "I am," or "That won't work," or they simply won't do what you tell them to because they think they already have it figured out.

Without counsel, plans go awry, but in the multitude of counselors, they are established."
Proverbs 15:22

———

...in a multitude of counselors, there is safety.
Proverbs 24:6

The disciples were a teachable people, and they sat at their Teacher's feet and sought wisdom. They were more than just followers; they were seekers.

Now it came to pass, as He was praying in a certain place, when He ceased that one of His disciples said to Him, "Lord teach us to pray"...
Luke 1:1

They didn't just passively receive from Him, they sought His wisdom. We would do well to learn from their example. They understood the importance of sitting at their Teacher's feet for the purpose of receiving and learning. We need to humble ourselves and subject ourselves to our own Pauls.

I personally have several Pauls in my life, and have had some come in and out for particular seasons. While Kate is my main mentor, there have been times that I have intentionally sat under other more seasoned believers for the purpose of learning more. I highly respect those who are ahead of me in their walk, and I honor them. Furthermore, I have learned the importance of being an "Elisha" and the blessing of the double portion that comes through serving those who are seasonably ahead of me.

...Timothy, our brother and minister of God, and our fellow laborer in the gospel of Christ...
1 Thess. 3:2

The word minister here is "diakonos" in the Greek (which is where we get the word deacon), but it means to run errands, to be an attendant, to serve in the menial tasks of life, to be a waiter. A little bit different than what we would expect. But God looks highly upon those who lay themselves at the feet of others and humble themselves through service. This has been a huge part of growing me to where I am, and I still very much enjoy the position of serving others and positioning myself "beneath" them. There is much reward in that, although the reward is not my motive.

We learn that a big part of being a Paul requires sacrifice and service, and we learn this as we serve our own Pauls first. Elisha washed the hands of Elijah before he got the double portion, David served Saul before he became king, Jacob served Laban before he possessed his own land, Joseph served Pharaoh before he was appointed lord of Egypt, and countless other examples of how serving and submitting raises you into your own spiritual position and anointing.

Loyalty and Faithfulness

But Elisha said, "As the Lord lives, and as your soul lives, I will not leave you!"
2 Kings 2:2

———

But Ruth said, "Entreat me not to leave you, Or turn back from following after you; For wherever you go, I will go; wherever you lodge, I will lodge"...
Ruth 1:16

One of the character traits that I think has gotten lost in today's culture is loyalty. Loyalty is at the very heart of God, because He is the essence of faithfulness. He is faithful even to the faithless, and His love remains loyal to us even when we are not loyal to Him. This is an important character trait, because it is what makes a person trustworthy. These are the kinds of people we are all looking for! I believe that in sitting under and serving others we learn much about walking in faithfulness, loyalty, and trustworthiness.

Elisha declares his loyalty to Elijah three times, but he also follows through on it! On a fun note, it was his faithfulness that earned him the double portion. One of the things I say a lot is that there are many who have faith, but there are few who are faithful. I love to have younglings around me that I can count on. I can count on the ones who are loyal and faithful, not necessarily to me, but rather to the mission and the call of their particular role. The ones who follow through are the ones to whom I will give the greater assignments.

He who is faithful in what is least is faithful also in much; and he who is unjust in what is least is unjust also in much.
Luke 16:10

———

His lord said to him, 'Well done, good and faithful servant; you have been faithful over a few things, I will make you ruler over many things…'
Matthew 25:21

And he said to him, 'Well done, good servant; because you were faithful in a very little, have authority over ten cities.'
Luke 19:17

God uses our role as Timothys to teach us how to be faithful and loyal to people and thus the work we are called to accomplish. Discipleship requires us to be faithful and love others often without gratefulness or any earthly return. Our disciples need to know that they can count on us, no matter what.

Learning from God

If any of you lacks wisdom, he should ask God who gives generously to ALL without finding fault...
James 1:5

Being a Timothy means not just seeking counsel from man but also from God Himself. Sometimes, we get stuck being a Timothy to man, and we never learn how to hear from God for ourselves. This is why it is important that we never give our disciples the answers, but rather teach them how to seek God for their answers. This passage in James goes on to talk about the man who is double-minded and unstable in all he does.

I think sometimes we are double-minded and unstable simply because we are seeking the advice of too many people and not looking to God to be our source of wisdom. The Word tells us that we have the mind of Christ and that the wisdom of God has been deposited into us through the Holy Spirit and that the Holy Spirit Himself will teach us all things.

But the anointing which you have received from Him abides in you, and you do not need that anyone teach you; but as the same anointing teaches you concerning all things, and is true, and is not a lie, and just as it has taught you, you will abide in Him.
1 John 2:27

We must recognize the power of the Holy Spirit within us to counsel and guide us. This word "abide" means to tarry, remain in, to be constant. There is a power that tarries within us that we need to tap into. It is as we recognize and rely upon His Presence that abides in us, that we come to abide in Him.

If you abide in Me, and My words abide in you, you will ask what you desire and it shall be done for you…by this My Father is glorified, that you bear much fruit; so you be my disciples.
John15:7

———

Then Jesus spoke to those Jews who believed Him, 'If you abide in My word, you are My disciples indeed. And you shall know the truth, and the truth shall make you free.'
John 8:31&32

There is much freedom that we gain when we tarry with the Lord and live in accordance to His Word. Being a disciple means that we sit at the Father's feet and drink of His Presence and His love and we eat of His Word. There are some things that man simply cannot reveal to you, but rather only the Holy Spirit can.

Paul prays for the saints of Ephesus.

…that the God of our Lord Jesus Christ, the Father of glory, may give to you the spirit of wisdom and revelation in the knowledge of Him.
Ephesians 1:17

There is much understanding that will come as we commune with God. There was a time in my life when the Lord revealed to me that strategies and answers would flow out of my intimacy and communion with Him, that He would reveal much to me as I sought HIM and not just answers from Him. It is supernatural, and it can't be explained, but I have experienced much freedom in just tapping into the Holy Spirit within and allowing His wisdom to be loosed and revealed to my mind.

Deep calls unto deep at the noise of Your waterfalls; All Your waves and billows have gone over me. The Lord will command His loving kindness in the daytimes and in the night His song shall be with me – a prayer to the God of my life.
Psalm 42:7&8

*The Spirit Himself bears witness with our sprit that we are
children of God.*
Romans 8:16

———

*And with many such parables He (Jesus) spoke the Word to them
as they were able to hear it. But without a parable He did not
speak to them. And when they were alone He explained all things
to His disciples.*
Mark 4:34

It was in during the disciples' private fellowship with
Jesus that Truth was revealed. Jesus explained it and
"connected the dots" so that their minds could comprehend
the parables in a way that was relevant to their lives. This is
a great picture of how the "logos" word became a "rhema"
word. These are two different Greek words to describe
what kind of word you are receiving. The logos word
typically refers to an utterance or simply a written word,
whereas rhema refers more to a revealed or "now" word
meaning it is relevant to you in your current situation.
There are times when I read something in the Scriptures
that I have read many times, but, for whatever reason, at
that moment it comes to life and becomes relevant to me.
That is a rhema word, and it is only because of the role of
the Holy Spirit. It is an "Ah ha" moment, but it comes
through my own fellowship with God.

There is much that cannot be received mind to mind but

can only come through revealed knowledge via the Holy Spirit who abides within us. But, we must learn to tap into Him and spend time with Him and be discipled by Him.

Jesus' Example

Even Jesus was intentional to commune with the Father. He sat daily at His Father's feet and served Him first in all that He did.

And early in the morning, while it was still dark, He arose and went out and departed to a lonely place, and was praying there.
Mark 1:35

————

And it was at this time that He went off to the mountain to pray, and He spent the whole night in prayer to God.
Luke 6:12

Jesus' fellowship with His Father was first. He knew the importance of knowing the Product before He went out to share the Product. His relationship with the Father preceded His assignments. He knew that it was through His own intimacy that His directives would come.

For I (Jesus) have given to them the words which You have given Me; and they have received them…
John 17:8

*Most assuredly, I say to you, the Son can do nothing of Himself,
but what He sees the Father do; for whatever He does, the Son also
does in like manner.*
John 5:19

———

*I can of Myself do nothing. As I hear, I judge; and My judgment
is righteous, because I do not seek My own will but the will of the
Father who send Me.*
John 5:30

Jesus made not a move and said not a word unless it
came from the Father…and He was OF the Father! If even
He was so intentional to pursue the heart of God, then
shouldn't we be as well? He demonstrated the idea of
being teachable and humbling Himself first. This is a great
example of being a Timothy!

No matter what season we are in, it is important to
recognize times when we must be a Timothy or need to be a
Timothy. There is always more to learn and God is
continuously growing us as His children. We must take
seriously the concept of being a disciple as Timothy was,
which is what will grow us into a Paul.

CHAPTER 8
WHAT DOES BEING A PAUL REQUIRE?

AS YOU NURTURE your own walk through your own discipleship, your life will begin to bear fruit. Cultivating the roots of a plant produces good and plentiful fruit, which is for the feeding of those around you. Sometimes we become selfish about our walk with the Lord, and we become fruit hoarders. But, we must recognize that the fruit in our lives is to be used for the good of those He brings into our lives.

Along the bank of the river, on this side and that, will grow all kinds of trees used for food; their leaves will not wither, and their fruit will not fail. They will bear fruit every month, because their water flows from the sanctuary. Their fruit will be for food, and their leaves for the medicine.
Ezekiel 47:12

This passage is saying that when we are deeply rooted by the river of God and entrenched in the Holy Spirit, our lives will produce fruit, no matter what season we are in. But the fruit is purposeful and is for the feeding and ministering to those around us. It is through discipleship that we teach others how to walk in healing. This requires us to let our disciples glean from us. This can be somewhat draining if we do not continually soak in the Living Water ourselves.

Let's get real here and talk about the nitty gritty details of what it really requires to pour our lives into another. After all, leading someone to the Lord only takes a moment, but discipleship takes a lifetime. This is more than just meeting with someone once a week or speaking into them during Sunday school.

When He has called the people to Himself, with His disciples also, He said to them, 'Whoever desires to come after Me, let him deny himself, and take up his cross, and follow Me. For whoever desires to save his life will lose it, but whoever loses his life for My sake and the gospel's sake will save it."
Mark 8:34&35

As I have traveled around teaching on discipleship, I have had people write down on index cards the top three things that they think discipleship requires. And while there are some great things listed, such as love, time, relationship, availability and accountability, I almost never see sacrifice, service and compassion listed.

Compassion

I want to look at compassion first, because it is compassion that should compel us to sacrifice and serve. If you look closely through the gospels, you will see that it was compassion that compelled Jesus to minister.

And when Jesus went out He saw a great multitude; and He was moved with compassion for them, and healed their sick.
Matthew 14:14

———

But when He saw the multitudes, He was moved with compassion for them because they were weary and scattered, like sheep having no shepherd.
Matthew 9:36

———

Then Jesus, moved with compassion, stretched out His hand and touched him, and said to him, "I am willing; be cleansed."
Mark 1:41

There was a time in my life when I really got convicted by the concept of compassion and began to ask the Lord what His heart of compassion looked like and felt like. I did all kinds of studies on the word compassion, but, when I discovered that the Greek word for compassion includes "to be moved in the inward parts" or "to have the bowels yearn," I realized that this was something I was not in tune with. It is the idea of having a deep physical reaction to the suffering of others.

Before I could move with compassion, I had to first recognize and repent that I had not experienced a Godly compassion. Those who know me know that I do not walk in mercy in the natural. But as I began to realize the power of compassion and how it is compassion that should compel us to minister, I began to cry out to God to loose His compassion for His people within me. And then I asked Him to show me what it looked like to execute compassionate acts…and I DID THEM!

I clearly remember God asking me to wash an elderly woman's feet in the middle of a youth event. I had no idea who this woman was or how it would be received, but I trusted what He was telling me to do, and I did it. As I did, my heart began to swell up with a supernatural compassion for this woman. I just remember weeping and weeping as I washed her feet. And when I was done, she looked into my eyes and said, "The Lord shows me that you have a true heart of compassion." I will never forget that moment. It was when the Lord manifested what was already IN me via the Holy Spirit. But the manifestation was activated by my faith and my obedience.

The Lord has put His heart of compassion into each of us as believers, but, unfortunately, our selfishness and pride will squelch that. Compassion demands that we step out of ourselves and reach out to others. It requires humility.

Let nothing be done through selfish ambition or conceit, but in lowliness of mind let each esteem others better than himself. Let each of you look out not only for his own interests, but also for the interests of others. Let this mind be in you which was also in Christ Jesus, who, being in the form of God, did not consider it robbery to be equal with God, but made Himself of no reputation, taking the form of a bondservant, and coming in the likeness of men. And being found in appearance as a man, He humbled Himself and became obedient to the point of death, even the death of the cross.
Phil. 2:3-8

Again, we see Jesus demonstrating the essence of humility for us through death. He was the ultimate sacrifice for us and wants us to sacrifice for those around us. But this is not a popular concept. The world has taught us to look out for ourselves. We have become like crabs in a bucket, each of us seeking our own good and willing to step on others to get to the top. But compassion will compel us to sacrifice, and discipleship requires sacrifice.

Sacrifice

I mentioned earlier in this book that the Lord at one point got a hold of my heart and really asked me what I was DOING to minister the gospel. It was as I was reading the story of the Good Samaritan that He began to convict me that I wasn't really doing anything to help people sacrificially. I had never really sacrificed in service of others.

I remember Him asking me, "Lisa, what separates you from the priest and the Levite?

What makes you different from them? They too saw the one who was beat up and stripped and left for dead, just like you do…so what makes you different from them?" Unfortunately, my answer was, "Not much." You see, both the priest and the Levite saw the man and recognized his need, but they were not willing to cross the road to DO something. Why not? They had no compassion. The Good Samaritan did!

*Now by chance a certain priest came down by the road. And when he saw him, he passed by on the other side. Likewise a Levite, when he arrived at the place, came and looked, and passed by on the other side. But a certain Samaritan, as he journeyed, came where he was, And when he saw him, **he had compassion.**"*
Luke 10:31-3

When I let the Lord really examine my heart, I realized that I was like the priest and the Levite who saw and maybe even felt sorry for the man, or maybe they prayed for him as they walked by, but ultimately, they did nothing. They were not willing to cross the road and give up their time, their safety, their reputation, their money, or their pride to actually get down in the dirt and get this man's blood on them.

Ugh, I can still feel the sting that this revelation brought that compelled a real travailing to my soul. I, too, was seeing on a daily basis people who were being stripped, beaten and left for dead.

I was seeing people who were being tattered by their circumstances, their emotions, their wounds, and their relationships; in other words, by the world and the devil. I began to see what Jesus saw when He looked out into the crowd and saw them as "harassed and helpless." This was not normal for me. There was such a compassion that rose up inside of me that I HAD to do something.

And instead of walking around saying, "Somebody oughta open up a shelter in Burleson" I started to feel the hand of God pressing upon my back saying, "How about you?! Are you available?" I will never forget it. It was life changing, and it is what started the shelter. It was HIS heart that compelled me to love sacrificially.

I am stressing this because true discipleship requires sacrifice. We must be willing to die to ourselves and give to others. And let me say this, it is not convenient. Don't wait until it is convenient. Most kids between the ages of 16-25 "kick in" after 11pm. If I had a quarter for every phone call or house visit I have gotten after 11pm, I would be a rich woman. This is not convenient, especially when you have small children or have just had a baby.

But it was during those time frames that a lot of these ladies were broken and ready to talk, and I wouldn't exchange them for anything. I am sure the Good Samaritan had other plans for his day, but he gave it all up to pour into the life of another. And don't forget that he did not just give up one day, but he went back to follow up on the man...because discipleship requires a lifetime.

Brad and I have opened up our home, our lives and our family to love and disciple others sacrificially...this means more than just spiritually ministering once a week, but also sacrificing time, energy, food, money, etc. I do not say this to boast but rather to share what is really required to disciple others with a Godly love. Love sacrifices. Period.

The truth is, of your own accord you will never have enough time, energy or resources to disciple the way Jesus did. But, when you are compelled by the heart of God there is always enough time, energy and resources to do His will, which is making disciples. When you are tapped into the heart of God, His compassion will swell up in you and you will sacrifice in ways you never thought you would, like opening up a shelter!

Consider with me Isaiah 58:6-11. The verses leading up to this passage reflect that God's people were practicing what they thought was fasting. But in actuality, their religious self-denial was simply just pretentious in that they were trying to "impress" God by works, while real needs of people were being ignored.

These people draw near to Me with their mouth, And honor Me with their lips, But their heart is far from Me. And in vain they worship Me, Teaching as doctrines the commandments of men. Matthew 15:8&9

I would be remiss if I didn't tell you that that passage

starts by Jesus addressing them as "hypocrites." This is what is happening in Isaiah 58, but Isaiah enlightens God's people by saying, "Listen up! I am going to give it to you straight...this is what pleases God."

"Is this not the fast that I have chosen: To loose the bonds of wickedness, To undo the heavy burdens, To let the oppressed go free, And that you break every yoke?
Is it not to share your bread with the hungry, And that you bring to your house the poor who are cast out; When you see the naked, that you cover him, And not hide yourself from your own flesh?
Isaiah 58:6&7

Ok, let's be honest before the Lord and let Him examine our lives. Are we doing this? Because this is the type of fasting that pleases the Lord and what He considers sacrifice. I believe this is one of the main reasons we don't see discipleship, because it requires this kind of selfless sacrifice. We have become a selfish culture, and I am not just talking about the pagans!

We can give up food all day long for days at a time, but if we aren't giving up our lives, what good is it? We MUST sacrifice more than just food, or TV, or whatever...we must sacrifice us! We need to shift from thinking like Abraham, who was willing to sacrifice Isaac, to being Isaac who was willing to BE sacrificed.

I beseech you therefore, brethren, by the mercies of God, that you present your bodies a living sacrifice, holy, acceptable to God, which is your reasonable service.
Romans 12:1

So let's take a look at the next couple of verses in Isaiah 58.

Then your light shall break forth like the morning, Your healing shall spring forth speedily, And your righteousness shall go before you; The glory of the Lord shall be your rear guard. Then you shall call, and the Lord will answer; You shall cry, and He will say, 'Here I am.' "If you take away the yoke from your midst, The pointing of the finger, and speaking wickedness, If you extend your soul to the hungry And satisfy the afflicted soul, Then your light shall dawn in the darkness, And your darkness shall be as the noonday. The Lord will guide you continually, And satisfy your soul in drought, And strengthen your bones; You shall be like a watered garden, And like a spring of water, whose waters do not fail.
Isaiah 58:8-11

What a beautiful promise this is! Look at the reward there is in living a life of sacrifice. Two verses exhorting us, followed up by verses of blessings. If we DO the first 2, then we will reap the following. While discipleship does indeed require sacrifice, what we get in return is incomparable. While my motive in discipling others is never to receive, I definitely do. This is the way the Lord works. As we pour into the lives of others, He restores us. I have received so much of my own healing by stepping outside of myself and discipling others sacrificially.

But, the devil will steal our own healing by keeping us focused on ourselves and living inwardly. He doesn't want us to put people before our schedules, or our laundry, or our work, or our...fill in the blank. But, God says that people are the most valuable of all creation and we should therefore be willing to sacrifice and lay down our lives for them.

Greater love has no one than this, than to lay down one's life for his friends.
John 15:13

Service

Discipleship requires service. After years of discipling His disciples, one of Jesus' final lessons to them was on servanthood. But, He didn't just talk to them about the importance of service, He demonstrated what it looks like by washing their feet. A menial task that would typically be done by the servant of the home was done by Jesus Himself.

There was no servant present and no one else assumed the role, so Jesus seized the opportunity to teach them what true service entailed. He took off His outer garment, a picture of removing pride, got down on His knees, a picture of going low, and got His hands dirty, a picture of meeting someone in their "yuck." This is a heart of a servant; one who is willing to serve in the low places, in the "dirty places", and with much humility. Imagine the impact of that moment; Jesus, the King of the world, bowing at the feet of others.

This is a great example of how demonstration can really drive a lesson home. He could have stood there and lectured them all night long on servanthood, He could have given them facts, all kinds of information, or even quoted the Word of God, but instead, He gave more than information, He executed by example.

For I have given you an example, that you should do as I have done to you. Most assuredly, I say to you a servant is not greater than his master; nor is he who is sent greater than he who sent him.
John 13:15&16

He executed information by being an example and then summed it all up by saying, by the way, you can know what being a servant means, but if you DO it, you will be blessed.

If you know these things, blessed are you if you do them.
John 13:17

We must be willing to do the same thing for our disciples. We can never think that we are greater than they are, speak down to them, or treat them as the lesser. But rather we must lower ourselves and serve them with much humility.

When we have to discipline ladies in our Home for breaking the covenant, one of the things I always say to them is, "We are not coming at you, but rather we are rallying around you." I want them to know that we are for them. I also typically ask them what we can be doing to serve them better and help them keep the covenant and fulfill their goals. Sounds ridiculous, but I genuinely want to own up to my part of why they might be falling, and I want to know how I can serve them better so that they succeed. This is not always easy, but it is important and necessary in raising up disciples. They must know that we are willing to go low, get dirty and humble ourselves for their advancement.

I would like to mention that when I find it hard to serve, I know that my heart is not in line with the Father's. If we are tapped into the love of God and believing it and walking in it ourselves, then service should be a joy and a blessing. Service that comes only out of duty will become drudgery and will account for nothing if it is not inspired by the Spirit.

...each one's work will become clear, for the Day will declare it, because it will be revealed by fire; and the fire will test each one's work, of what sort it is.
1 Corinthians 3:13

The Message says it this way,

Eventually there is going to be an inspection. If you use cheap or inferior materials, you'll be found out. The inspection will be thorough and rigorous. You won't get by with a thing.

Our service builds into the lives of others, but we would do well to make sure that our service is compelled by God and energized by the Holy Spirit. He is creative and innovative, and only He can know what kind of service will best minister to each heart that you are discipling. Don't settle for the inferior when God's ways are excellent and best.

The Heart of a Parent

Paul was more than just an advisor to Timothy; he depicted the heart of a parent to him.

I do not write these things to shame you, but as my beloved children I warn you. For though you might have ten thousand instructors in Christ, yet you do not have many fathers; for in Christ Jesus I have begotten you through the gospel. Therefore I urge you, to imitate me.
1 Corinthians 4:14&15

This verse is saying that there will be a plethora of people who advise with condemnation and criticism, but finding one who will be like a parent and advise us out of love, as well as open their lives up for imitation, will be few. Read it again in The Message.

I'm not writing all this as a neighborhood scold just to make you feel rotten. I'm writing as a father to you, my children. I love you and want you to grow up well, not spoiled. There are a lot of people around who can't wait to tell you what you have done wrong, **but there aren't many fathers willing to take the time and effort to help you grow up.** *It was as Jesus helped me proclaim God's Message to you that I became your father. I'm not, you know, asking you to do anything I'm not already doing myself.*

Discipleship requires the heart of a parent. There are many who are willing to speak truth into the lives of others, sometimes solicited and sometimes not, but there are few people who are willing to compassionately parent others through sacrifice and service. This is what will set you apart from all the others. When you are willing to love ALL THE TIME sacrificially and with much service. The way we love our disciples is our greatest demonstration and will be the example to them of living like Christ.

CHAPTER 9
GENERATIONAL
BARRIERS

I WANT to briefly touch on a huge barrier that I see in our culture, as well as in the church, that breaks down organic discipleship: generational differences. We have been taken captive into a worldview of generational gaps and are unable to see the beauty in which God intends for generational differences. God's economy is very different from the world's economy.

But you are a chosen generation, a royal priesthood, a holy nation, His own special people, that you may proclaim the praises of Him who called you out of darkness into His marvelous light.
1 Peter 2:9

Peter addresses believers here as one generation in God. No breakdown, no division, but rather a group who all come from the same place and are brought into the same place. In Christ, we are one generation, because there is no "age" of the Holy Spirit. Teens have the same Holy Spirit as adults, and adults the same as elders, and elders the same as children.

So we would do well to recognize that while we indeed do live in a world with many generations, it is all those generations that make up the body of Christ. Therefore, any place we see generational breakdowns, we can be assured that the power of the body is being handicapped.

Now, I know there are definite differences, but if we are walking in the Spirit, we would recognize these differences as completions and not hindrances. We would use the differences to strengthen us as a body, but instead I see it weakening us. Think of how much we could accomplish for the Kingdom if we pulled together the wisdom of the older generation, the resources of the middle generation, and the energy of the younger generation!

So, how does this play into discipleship? Well, discipleship requires that we learn to recognize and appreciate generational differences; strengths and weaknesses. All generations are in great need of each other to complete the work that God has called His corporate body to fulfill. One of the most revealing titles for Himself is "The God of Abraham, Isaac and Jacob." He is the God of all generations.

So, let's break this down and talk about what really keeps us from uniting across generations. I would like to say that I am safe in speaking to both the older and the younger since I fall right in the middle. So I will lump myself into both categories, since I am learning on both ends as well.

To the Older Generations

We must become more flexible and willing to adjust to fit today's younger generation. Often, we are so stuck in our ways that we are out of touch with what's really going on in society. We are clueless as to what the younger generation REALLY encounters on a daily basis. If you want to step outside your box, go to a high school sporting event, and just watch and listen and learn. Please do NOT go to judge or point your finger but rather with the intent learn how you can reach into that generation.

Go with love in mind. Remember, discipleship means going to where they are, meeting them in their environment for the purpose of loving them. We need to be willing to get outside our comfort zone and leave all judgment behind. As the older and wiser, it is our responsibility to go to where they are and not expect them to come to where we are.

We are also stuck in our methods. Let's be honest, we put tradition before relevance and methods before people. While God never changes His message, He DOES indeed change His methods! Why? Because He recognizes where people are, and He wants to be relevant to them. Reaching people with the message of love is more important than methods. We would do well to learn from the Master Himself and loosen our grip on our traditions and methods.

At Crazy8, we minister primarily to the unchurched. And though some have never been in church, others have, but were harshly judged or were hurt by someone in the church. Now, I realize that Truth itself can be offensive, but I am talking about people who were scolded by an elder for wearing a hat the first time they darkened the doors of church, or for carrying a cup of coffee, or for wearing tennis shoes.

My husband was once reproved by an elder for wearing cargo shorts to church. This breaks my heart, and we have no idea how it is turning the younger generation off. We must look beyond the outer appearance of a man and go to their hearts! Although there are indeed times when people show up wearing something inappropriate or behaving inappropriately, we must love them more than we love our rules.

Remember, it is the kindness of the Lord that leads to repentance (Romans 2:4). It is through relationship that you will earn you the right to speak truths in love. But unless we love them first, they might come in, but they will not stay.

I realize that it is hard to step outside of what we are familiar with, but Jesus addresses this when He talks about the wineskins.

And no one puts new wine into old wineskins; or else the new wine will burst the wineskins and be spilled, and the wineskins will be ruined. But new wine must be put into new wineskins,

and both are preserved. And no one, having drunk the old wine, immediately desires new; for he says, "The old is better."
Luke 5:37-39

The Pharisees were questioning and judging the methods of the disciples. They were inflexible and rigid and comfortable with the familiarity of the old wine, meaning old methods and religious traditions. But, new wine means the yeast within it is still active, alive and growing, and these Pharisees missed out on the energy and effervescence of the new wine. We too will miss out on the growth and movement of the Kingdom by rejecting new ideas and new methods that are relevant to the younger generation.

We are hindering the overall growth of the church because both the old wineskin AND the new wine are ruined when the old wineskins bursts. New wine will only develop into its richest state if it is encompassed by a new wine skin that will afford the wine growth and movement. A new wine skin is pliable, whereas an old wine skin is rigid and stiff, unable to stretch...or in our case unwilling to stretch. Look around your church and see if there are many youth and adolescents. If you don't see many, ask why.

We must own up to this, and while I think there is an extreme in becoming too "seeker friendly," there is some relevance to it as well. The younger generation is the future of the church...own up and do something!

I sit on a board of people in our community called The Character Council. This is a group of people who represent the city, the school district, the churches, and the chamber; four entities that come together and put two major events on each year to uphold the character and integrity of Burleson. It is very unique to our city and an incredible concept.

This group started some 18 years ago by people whom I would consider "icons" in our city. I have MUCH respect for them and their endeavors over the years, but what I respect the most is their willingness to change things up as some of us "younglings" have started sitting on this council. The message and mission of the group has not changed a bit, but some of the methods have. They are open to our suggestions and ideas that will make the council more effective to today's culture.

We as the younglings have no "rank" in this room, but the older generation has welcomed us and our ideas with MUCH excitement and the council has only grown more and more effective to our community. Moreover, we have gleaned from their wisdom and have been inspired by their work and passion for Burleson. Personally, I have learned much from these "icons," and I cannot think of any other board or council that I am more honored to be a part of! The church would do well to follow this example.

Another weakness of the older generation is apathy and a lack of unction for life in general. We have grown tired and weary and often say things like, "I've done my time." But here is what I have to say to that, "It you aren't dead, you aren't done!" God has a plan for you every day of your life, from birth to death…but we grow apathetic and comfortable, and our effectiveness for the kingdom is thus weakened.

We must decide to actively re-engage in today's culture. Energy will come to you as you serve, trust me! Some of our most effective staff members are over the age of 70, and they will tell you that they are energized by the work of the Lord. But the devil would have you settle into a state of apathy and selfishness, which will only nurture fatigue and weariness.

I also hear the older generation say, "I have nothing to offer." NOT TRUE! You have experience to offer. I often say that life has two teachers, wisdom and consequences. Wisdom is when we glean from the mistakes of others, while consequences is when we learn from our own mistakes. In both cases, we will learn, but how beautiful it is when we can learn before we fall instead of through a fall because we have gleaned from another's experience. Our trips into and through the valley can be greatly diminished through the wisdom of the older generation. The older are thus very valuable to the growth of the Kingdom and the younger need them.

The Younger Generation

Now that I have "picked on" the older generation, let me shift to the younger.

Remember the days of old, consider the years of many generations. Ask your father, and he will show you; Your elders,

and they will tell you.
Deuteronomy 32:7

We need to recognize that we can learn from the former generations. Let's go back to the concept of wisdom and consequences. Wisdom is available to us in the former generations, and though it is true that the older may not make themselves available to the younger, it is also true that the younger do not value the wisdom that the older generation has.

Often the younger have a "know it all" attitude and do not think they need to learn from others, especially those not of their generation. We tend to be haughty and unteachable. This, combined with the fact that we can gain information from technology, keeps us from looking to and gleaning from those who have actually experienced what we haven't. Let's call this what it is...pride. Pride will keep you thinking that you already know everything.

When given counsel from an elder, even when I think I know, I have learned not to say, " I know," or "I am already doing that," or "that won't work," and I definitely NEVER correct them, in fact I would not correct anyone in a public setting. But, I try to always take the position of looking inward and trusting that they know something I don't, and I want to learn from this. This is not always easy.

There was a time several years ago when I was doing one of the few Bible studies I have ever done with a group of primarily older women. There were a few women in the study who were what I would call "legalistic" and bound by some of their theologies. I would openly share my views and was very passionate about sharing Scriptures. After one of the meetings, the leader came to me in love and said some of the ladies were offended, because I was too "Aggressively confident about the Scriptures."

I did not understand this, and I wanted to say, "Why thank you, yes, I am!" I didn't see why this was wrong, and it would have been easy for me to have taken up an offense and never gone back. But, the Holy Spirit compelled me to let Him search me and refine me through their words. And guess what? I learned a lot. For one, I learned that sometimes it is best to say nothing, especially when I do not have the rank in the room. Two, He taught me that when I do speak to adjust my body language, and my tone of voice so that I would be heard more lovingly and tender.

He showed me how physically leaning forward in my passion could be perceived as aggressive and combative. This was certainly NOT what I was intending. But had I not taken the time to respect that maybe they saw something I didn't, I would have never learned how to know my "audience" and shape my message so that it is better received. This included not just the words that I spoke, but the way I spoke and also my body language.

We, as the younger, have also lost the concept of recognizing the rank of elders and therefore often lack a general respect. Somewhere respect of our elders has gotten lost. When I am in a room full of elders, I am typically very quiet. I want to, first of all, respect them by not talking out of turn, and I also understand that I must earn the right to "speak." If my opinion is not sought, I often won't give it, or I will seek "permission" before I do.

I want to soak up all I can from them by listening and learning from the wisdom in the room. I also respect them by serving them. Throwing out their garbage, opening doors for them, picking up what they drop, carrying things, and honoring them with words and actions. This is not because they are old but rather because they have earned the right to be respected. Most of our younglings treat those of us who are older in this manner, because they see us doing the same with each other and with those older than us.

A weakness of the younger generation is that they often lack self-control or self-restraint. They don't know how to set a pace and tend to over commit and under fulfill. In other words, they tend to lack faithfulness in their commitments. This is due to their mindset of "taking on the world," which, if controlled or monitored or submitted to an older person for review, can be a GREAT strength.

Yoking Two Oxen

When a farmer would yoke two oxen together, they would typically couple an older ox with a younger ox. They used the older ox to teach and train the younger to stay focused and set a pace. The younger ox was typically full of energy and had much strength, but, in their youthfulness, they would expend all their energy in the first half of the work and, therefore, would wear out quickly. This is just like I described above.

A younger person will often become so passionate they will commit too much and give it all they have for a certain amount of time, but then they will quickly burnout. So, the older is needed to help set a pace and teach self-control and discipline in actually completing and following through on their commitments.

On the other side of the yoke, the older ox lacks energy and vigor to complete the job on their own. But, they are able to pull from the strength and energy of the younger. Again, the same is true of us. I have many elders on my staff who say they can't keep up with me, because I have so much energy and passion.

It is the fiery part of me that energizes them in the ministry and keeps them excited and passionate, but they help me set a pace and stay disciplined. Sometimes, in my passion, I get ahead of God and start forcing my way instead of waiting on God…in such times, just like the young ox, I grow tired and weary and am unable to finish strong.

How marvelous it would be and how many more fields could we plow if we would recognize our strengths and how they complete each other's weaknesses. This is what discipleship does, it organically nurtures such connections which make us a more powerful and effective body for His Kingdom. May we restore generational gaps and be united as one generation, God's generation; the God of Abraham, Isaac and Jacob.

CHAPTER 10
THE GOAL OF
DISCIPLESHIP

SO, what is our goal in discipleship, our mission statement if you will? I have thought a lot about that, and there are many things we want to strive for when discipling someone. Of course, one of the things I want to accomplish in discipleship is discipling someone to the place of them discipling someone else. This is not necessarily a matter of adequacy as much as it is urgency. I want them to catch the heart of discipleship and be "urged" to do the same.

I often ask this question during our discipleship conferences; "When was the last time you discipled someone to the place where they could turn around and disciple another person?" It saddens me to tell you that I almost never have anyone raise their hand. Why is this? Well, going back to what we discussed earlier in regard to being passionate about your product...if we are discipling someone in their own walk with the Lord, would they not

just automatically turn around and do the same? Most of
our "younglings" at Crazy8 are biting at the bit to disciple
someone younger than they are, whether they are "ready"
or not. They are eager, because they want others to
experience what they have through their own discipleship
relationship. My own relationship with Kate is what
impressed me to disciple others. I know how it impacted
my own life and how desperately I needed it. Kate didn't
have to tell me to go do the same or teach me how…I just
did! The point is, most of us don't disciple others to this
point, because we aren't discipling others at all.

That being said, let's narrow the goal down a little more
and make it a little more individualized. Here is what I
want to see personally when I come alongside a disciple. I
want to see them come into the fullness of life, and the
fullness of their own anointing.

The Fullness of Life

One of the things that breaks my heart is seeing people
not reaping the fullness of life, even as believers. A lot of
times, we think we are, but we aren't. Part of the problem is
that we don't know enough about what the fullness of life
means, and we don't know what is due us as believers. I
don't want to tangent off too deeply into this, because it
could be its own book, but I do want to touch on it.

Like the Israelites, many of us have been given freedom
through Christ, but we get stuck wandering around the
wilderness and never step into the promise land. But the

fullness of life is in the promise land…the place where the milk and honey flows abundantly. And, although the Lord was with the Israelites in the wilderness in that He never left them, He provided for them, and He loved them, the Israelites were not stepping into what God really had in mind for them.

This is too often what we are like today. We get stuck, or sometimes even are just satisfied with the wilderness and we never move beyond our fears, our doubts, our addictions, our anger, or …fill in the blank! Some of us would even rather go back to our captivity, because it is familiar and comfortable.

The mission statement for Crazy8 Ministries is: *A ministry compelled by the love of Christ to reach out and come alongside others and bring healing to the body, soul an Spirit; offering wholeness in yesterday, providing help in today, for a victorious walk in tomorrow.*

In a nutshell, we are a ministry committed to healing others body, soul and spirit. We want to see people step into the promise land and reap the fullness of life that was given to them on the cross. Everyone is at a different place in their healing process that brings them to whole living, or living in the fullness. While some have never received salvation, others have, yet are plagued with what we call sick thinking, or they suffer from sick emotions, or they continue to make sick choice after sick choice. This means their soul is sick. Even those who are saved must learn how to think, feel and choose in a healthy manner. This is a huge part of the discipleship process. Coming alongside others and teaching them how to walk out their salvation.

Therefore, my beloved, as you have always obeyed, not as in my presence only, but now much more in my absence, work out your own salvation with fear and trembling...
Phil. 2:12

This "working" portion is referring to the sanctification of our soul. Getting our soul caught up to the life that we have been given spiritually by the Holy Spirit. We call it lining up our thoughts, emotions, and choices with God's. While our spirits are supernaturally justified by Jesus, our soul realm needs some "working out."

Not that I have already attained, or am already perfected; but I press on, that I may lay hold of that for which Christ Jesus has also laid hold of me. Brethren, I do not count myself to have apprehended; but one thing I do, forgetting those things which are behind and reaching forward to those things which are ahead, I press toward the goal for the prize of the upward call of God in Christ Jesus.
Phil. 3:12-14

This is probably one of my favorites of all the Scriptures, because it shows Paul understanding that he needs to continually be pressing in toward who he is in the Spirit. He recognizes that until we reach eternity, our soul will continue to "lag behind" our spirit, and he rises up and commits to grabbing hold of the fullness of who he is in Christ. This means living in accordance to what is set before us and not behind us.

Often, we as believers don't realize the fullness of life we are missing out on. Our "thinkers, feelers and pickers" (mind, emotion, and will) have been molded by our circumstances, the world, other people, and even our own perceptions, understanding, and intellect instead of the Truth of Jesus. These are often things in our past, which is why Paul is urging us to forget the past. Our personalities have often been molded by everything other than who we REALLY are in Christ. This is why a huge goal of discipleship is to retrain the soul...it's the sanctification process.

All Scripture is given by inspiration of God, and is profitable for doctrine, for reproof, for correction, for instruction in righteousness, that the man of God may be complete, thoroughly equipped for every good work.
2 Timothy 3:16&17

Verse 16 talks about how the Word of God can profit the soul of a man. I think we are very good at the first three that are listed...and the church is good a teaching that part, but the fourth one, "instruction for righteousness" is where we often fall short. Let's look at it in The Message.

Every part of Scripture is God-breathed and useful one way or another – showing us truth, exposing our rebellion, correcting our mistakes, training us to live God's way.

The training toward righteousness requires action. It is where we don't just hear the truth or feel the sting of reproof and the call to change, but we actually DO something to retrain ourselves. If you read this phrase in the Greek it includes the concept of "cultivating the soul." That nails it! My goal in discipling another is to teach and show them how to cultivate their soul to line up with the Holy Spirit.

The rest of the verse takes us into the second goal, which is seeing your disciple come into the fullness of their anointing.

Stepping Up and Stepping In

...that the man of God may be complete, thoroughly equipped for every good work.
2 Timothy 3:17

God has a work for each of us within His kingdom. He has a call on each of our lives, and there is a purpose that each of us fill. But, the great thing is that He has also equipped us to fulfill this call.

His divine power has given to us all things that pertain to life and godliness...
2 Peter 1:3

As we work with our disciple and watch them come more and more into the fullness of their healing and life, you will notice that they will begin to have more unction about their life. One of our roles is to recognize their anointing and help them step into it. There is nothing more rewarding than watching someone else blossom into who they have always been wired to be! Just like a seed has everything in it to become the plant that it is called to be, so are we like that. God put into us from the very beginning the "genetics" to bloom into who He created us to be.

One of the things that we can learn from Jesus is that He looked at people according to who they were in the Spirit. He did not identify them by their circumstances or their failures, but rather, He identified them by their potential. We see this same example clear back in the Old Testament. God calls Abram "The Father of many nations" long before Abram bears any children. He was barren, but yet God called him fruitful.

Think about Gideon in Judges 6, he defines himself by the fact that he is from the weakest clan and in fact is the least in his father's house. And, I would have to say that these facts have defined his personality as well in that he is cowardly when God first calls him. But God sees something else, He sees a "mighty man of valor." And, He gives him an assignment based on who He knows Gideon REALLY is. Same thing with Mary, she refers to herself as a maidservant in a lowly state. But God calls her, "Highly favored one." He gives her an assignment as well, that seems impossible. But look at His response when she, too, questions her ability to fulfill the call that is on her life.

*The Holy Spirit will come upon you and the power of the Highest
will overshadow you…For with God nothing will be impossible.
Luke 1:35&37*

God sees our potential in accordance with the power of
the Holy Spirit within us, and we need to learn to do the
same with our disciples. Remember the one-two punch?
This is where it comes in, we see their anointing, and we
provide opportunities for them to step into that anointing.
This means we are challenging them beyond the soul and
forcing them to step into the Spirit.

Our Outreach Ministry Coordinator has some fabulous
event planning skills, and she had been doing it for a
secular industry for several years before she came to
Crazy8. We have an annual festival that we put on in our
community called City on a Hill, and she is the main
coordinator for that event. I have worked with her over the
past years in building her confidence, particularly in
building relationships and communicating with people that
we are partnering with to grow the event each year.

She is very talented administratively and has a lot of
natural organizational skills. But, the Lord gave me eyes to
see beyond her talent and into her anointing. This past
year, I really pushed her out in front and encouraged her to
get "ahead of me" in the planning. My schedule has gotten
more and more stretched with the growth of the ministry,
and the event has grown, so I needed her to "go!" And she
needed me to push her. I found myself saying to her
continuously, "Green light, Liz…go girl go!"

And guess what, she blossomed, and the event was incredibly successful and effective! The best part for me was watching her cry the day of the event as she looked around and saw the fruit of her anointing. Although she may have been surprised, I was not...and I still see even more in her!

I have had the pleasure of having so many elders speak "big" into me, and while there have been times it has freaked me out, most of the time, I have been challenged and encouraged. But, it was not just words, it was opportunities that came with those words to step up and step in. I cannot tell you how many times I have had one of those elders call me on the carpet and have me pray for a stranger, or minister healing, or sing a song, or preach spur of the moment. I have even had some fly me places to minister...all because they saw what God was doing in me and through me long before I saw it.

This should be our goal, to see our disciples step into their potential. This is our goal with the ladies in our Home, as well. These ladies are so broken they can't even imagine living their dreams, in fact most of them don't even dare to dream anymore because life has crushed them and the devil has stolen their vision.

Where there is no revelation, the people cast off restraint...
Proverbs 29:18

The Word of God is clear in many places that lack of vision and purpose will discourage and destroy people.

When we have no vision, we lose hope in our future. One of the things I love to do is have our ladies go back to when they were a child and consider all that they wanted to be when they grew up. After all, no one says, I want to be homeless when I grow up, or I want to be an addict, or I want to be stuck in a pit of debt and depression. Of course not, we sit around as children dreaming big dreams...with the faith of a child. This is what I want to tap into with our ladies. I want to give them permission to dream again, find out what has always been in them, and then work with them day after day to bring them to that place.

We currently have one lady in our home who has always been able to fix things, particularly cars. She loves getting her hands dirty and working under a hood. After we worked her past her fears and anxieties, and she started seeing her identity in Christ, she enrolled in automotive school...and she loves it. She will graduate soon, and she is soaring! She has stepped up and stepped in...I love it!

Mini-Me

Now, I want to insert in here that our disciples are not called to look like us. Kate is also writing a book right now, and one of the chapters is all about not making "mini mes."

She writes...

For we are not bold to class or compare ourselves with some of those who commend themselves; but when they measure

themselves by themselves and compare themselves with themselves, they are without understanding.
2 Cor 12:10

———

"Each of us do it. We look at our lives and view ourselves as the standard of what is best. If we are extroverted, we think that is the better way to be. If we don't allow dating, we think everyone should agree. If we are teachers, we assume that it should be everyone's goal to teach. It goes on and on.
With discipling, things are no different. Our tendency is to view our spiritual lives, our passions, our giftings, our vision as the standard to which we are building those we disciple.
One of the very hardest things to do is to help them grow into who God is making them to be, not into a Mini Me.
I think the #1 thing I've learned is that the most vital part of discipling others is discernment. We need to be discerning where God is working in our disciple. We need to discern their bent, as the verse we so often use for our children says.
Train up a child in the way he should go, even when he is old he will not depart from it.
Prov 22:6

My understanding of the Hebrew words translated "the way he should go" is better expressed "according to his bent", or how he is designed. Our oldest daughter was bent toward reading and directing from an early age. We could see, even when she was 12 months old, that language was more than a skill for her, it was a joy. She was always writing and arranging plays for her siblings from the time she was four. So, throughout her schooling we geared things around this great strength of hers. And now her degree and desired profession is to teach acting and freelance writing.

Are you following my thought pattern here? OUR job is to find the bent or the leaning of our disciple and help grow them in that strength. We cannot assume our strength will be theirs. Although the reality is that they will learn from our strength and it will be multiplied in their life as well. That is OK so long as we remember that WE are not the goal. God's design for THEM is the goal.

Again discernment is the key. We listen, we watch, we pray. We learn to understand them inside and out. Listening to the Spirit is vital or we end up with arrogance and haughtiness behind our vision for them. We pray that the Lord lets us see them as He sees them. And we pray continually for compassionate and loving hearts. Trust me on this, there is a lot of Truth we can say to someone who knows we love them unconditionally and are not judging them!"

One of the things that I have always appreciated about Kate is that she raised me up to step into MY anointing. Kate and I could not be more different. To name a few, Kate has a personal conviction of wearing a head covering anytime she is worshipping or praying and when she goes to church. She also does not believe in speaking out loud in front of the church as a woman. This is hugely different than me.

I definitely do not wear a head covering, and you can't shut me up at the pulpit. I am an ordained minister, and I love to preach the gospel anywhere and everywhere the Lord allows me to. Kate has never once tried to make me look like her; in fact, she has had more confidence in me than I have had in myself. And other than my husband, she has been my number one support. I know that she saw all God was doing long before I saw it, and she groomed me for HIS call not hers.

So Saul clothed David with his armor, and he put a bronze helmet on his head; he also clothed him with a coat of mail. David fastened his sword to his armor and tried to walk, for he had not tested them. And David said to Saul, "I cannot walk with these, for I have not tested them." So David took them off. Then he took his staff in his hand, and he chose for himself five smooth stones from the brook, and put them in a shepherd's bag, in a pouch which he had, and his sling was in his hand. And he drew near to the Philistine.
1 Samuel 17:38-40

Saul tried to throw his armor on David, not realizing that it was not fit for David, but rather was fit for Saul. David had his own weapon that the Lord had equipped him with, and it was not like Saul's. This is a great example of how we all have our own equipping, and we should not throw our armor on our disciples...nor should we allow anyone else to throw theirs on us. I have had many people who have told me that I have this person's mantel or that person's...or that I have an anointing like this person or that, but God has made an armor that is fit for me. And, He has given me my own weapons to fight the Goliaths I face, and He has taught me how to use them.

Our goal is not to conform others by our image but rather to see them transformed by HIS image. We want to see them reap the fullness of life and the fullness of who He is. As they come into this knowledge of who He is, and the power He has put within them, they will step up and step into their own anointing.

As an example, I often discuss a scene from the end of the movie "Facing the Giants" where the coach is counteracting the mentality of the team. They are convinced that they can't beat their next opponent and they see themselves as losers, but he knows they are winners. His goal is to see them step up and step into the fullness of their potential and be victorious. So the coach picks the leader of the team and challenges him to bear crawl down the field as long as he can.

He puts the weight of another player on his back and then blindfolds him so that he has to rely solely upon the voice of the coach to guide him. As they are starting out the challenge, he asks the player how far he thinks he can go. In other words, he is asking, "What do you think your fullest potential is?" The player gives an answer, and the coach quickly says, "I think you can do more!" And then he says, "Promise me you'll give it all you got!" And the next few minutes of this scene display one of the most intense, yet best demonstrations of discipleship that I have found. A coach who loves this player enough to go on the field with him, get low and crawl with this kid all the way across the finish line.

As the player begins to get fatigued and grow weary, the coach roots the kid on hard by yelling things like, "I know it hurts, I know it burns, but keep going, keep going, don't give up, give it all you got, give it all you got!" Through this scene, we see the other players, who were making fun of the player, now standing and rooting him on with amazement at how far he was going. When the player finally collapses with fatigue, the coach takes his blindfold off. He is shocked to see that he made it farther than he ever thought he could go, and he was in the end zone.

This is it! The goal is to give it all we've got and accomplish all we can be. But without our own "coach" coming along side us and rooting us through the "burn" of the weight we must bear, how can we cross the finish line? I cannot tell you how many times I have had a mentor literally root me through times of wanting to give up.

Early in my ministry at Crazy8, I experienced a personal betrayal that stung so badly, I literally got up and left my office. I emotionally quit the ministry all together and just got up and left without telling anyone. I went home and turned off my phone and shut the world out. I spent the day wrestling with God and begging Him to cut me loose of the ministry. It was too painful and the loss I was experiencing because of it was too great for me at that moment.

I was like the player on the field who was feeling the sting and was unable to go another step. It was about 11:30pm that night when I heard a knock on my bedroom door followed by the voice of my ministry intercessor who said, "Lisa, it's me, Shirley, and I am coming in." Shirley is our 76-year-old prayer warrior who spiritually guides me and speaks into me specifically with the ministry. She has been with me and has in so many ways discipled me through much of the growth of Crazy8. Well, the Lord alerted her that night to come and minister to me.

I was angry that she was there, because I was content to wallow in my misery and hurt. She was unwavering in her passion to see me get up from this and she came boldly to the side of my bed. She leaned over and said one word, "Overcomer." And then she hugged me as I cried, and then she got up and left. That was it! But I promise you that had she not come to where I was and challenged me by what she saw, I would have quit.

I could give you example after example of how God has used my mentors to bring me to where I am. And, He still does. I want to get to the end of my life and say with confidence, "I gave it all I had!"

CONCLUSION

I pray that this book has redefined your thoughts on discipleship and challenged you to allow the Holy Spirit to search your heart on this topic. My prayer is that you will move from information to execution and that your life will not speak, but will BE.

That you will not be satisfied with knowing the Word, but rather desire for the Word to be made flesh in you and the way you live your life. See Him, live Him, and teach Him!

"There is always time to do the will of God" – Kate Megill

"Always do the right thing" – Pastor Gloria Gillaspie

"There is no limit on what the Lord can do if you don't care who gets the credit." – Pastor Gloria Gillaspie

"Never get so busy being a minister that you forget to minister" – Pastor Mark Hewitt

"People are God's most valuable creation" – Pastor Gary Burkins

"Wherever you go, just take them with you" - Pastor Rick Eubanks

WORKS CITED

New Spirit Filled Life Bible, New King James Verson. Jack Hayford, Executive Editor. Thomas Nelson Bibles, 2002.

The Message Bible. Eugene H. Peterson. NavPress Publishing Group, 1993.

The Blue Letter Bible. www.blueletterbible.org. 1995.

Megill, K. (2014) *Silver Threads: Weaving godly wisdom into the lives of younger women*. Publisher: Author

ABOUT CRAZY8 MINISTRIES

Mission: A ministry compelled by the love of Christ to reach and come alongside others and bring healing to the body, soul and spirit; offering wholeness in yesterday, providing help in today, for a victorious walk in tomorrow.

Crazy8 Ministries was founded in 2011 and started as a conference ministry where founder, Lisa Schwarz, designed and developed conferences and travelled around the United States preaching and teaching the gospel in many arenas. It was her desire to offer more than just a "weekend experience." With people contacting her in need of further ministry, the ministry evolved into what is now the Crazy8 Ministries facility, located in Burleson, TX.

Because each person is at a different place in the healing process of living out the fullness of the gospel, there are several different arms of the ministry. Each arm helps to accomplish the mission through its own unique focus and partner together with one heart and one mind for one purpose: to meet the needs of each person that is served. The goal is to bring those served into the wholeness of Jesus

Christ and move them into a place of thriving, body, soul, and spirit.

The Welcome Home Ministry (WHM) is a long term home for women and their children who are in a "sick circumstance" and offer the hope, help and freedom of Jesus Christ in a practical way through a loving, secure, multi-family home. The WHM is an 18-24 month restorative program that is designed to come alongside to provide emotional, spiritual, and physical help in their today, meeting them right where they are.

The Biblical Counseling/Discipleship Ministry (BCDM) focuses on ministering to those who suffer from "sick thinking or sick emotions" through one-on-one free counseling and discipleship as well as group opportunities. The BCDM comes alongside others in order to instill hope, healing, and life transformation through the power of the Holy Spirit and the Word of God, so they may live victoriously in Jesus Christ.

The Outreach Ministry focuses on serving and providing opportunities within our community in order to build relationships and touch others with the love of Christ and the transforming power of the gospel; working toward city transformation by promoting unity and oneness of heart, to proclaim that we are a city of one King.

The Conference Ministry (CM) focuses on going out and inviting others to come and see who Jesus is and experience the healing He has for them. The CM offers many services around the setting of a conference/retreat designed with the particular and unique needs of the organization in mind.

To learn more about Crazy8 Ministries, visit www.crazy8ministries.com

ABOUT THE AUTHOR

Lisa Schwarz is a nationally recognized speaker, bestselling author, Certified Biblical Counselor, Professional Life Coach, Brain Health Coach, and Founder/CEO of Crazy8 Ministries.

A premier event planner, Lisa delivers her impactful message nationwide at conferences, workshops, and home experiences. Enforcing purpose: maximizing who you are, what you do and cultures around you is the passion that drives her. Lisa is uniquely experienced as a disciple-maker to individuals, mentor to groups and expert leader for developing restorative housing programs.

Equipping and empowering others to experience transformation through Jesus Christ guides her purpose for *community* and belief in the power of unity; *together we are better.* Lisa is available for sharing her experience, education and expertise with others engaged with improving life for other people.

She and her husband, Brad, reside in Texas, and have 6 children, and a daughter and son-in-law.

ALSO BY LISA SCHWARZ

Mastering Your Seasons

To Love and To Be Loved

Enforcing You: Activating Your Kingdom Identity In Christ

Enforcing Purpose

Enforcing Prayer

Come and See: Come and See: The Jesus Approach to Equipping
Biblical Disciples

Made in the USA
Columbia, SC
14 September 2022

67055475R00096